Copyrigl

Photography by Brian Metters unless otherwise attributed

Cover design by: Danell Nelson

Internal artwork: Danell Nelson

Contents

Introduction

This is the way to learn about wine ...... through experiences, whether you are young or old, a traveller or a "stay at home" or a WSET student. This book is not a wine guide, nor is it a travel guide. It is a memoir of our wine experiences over half a century from student days to retirement and old age. Certainly this book involves and includes travel, mostly across the wine regions of France especially Burgundy, Loire, and Alsace which are our three favourite places to visit. But we have also "engaged" with wine in USA, Italy, Spain and Hungary too, often at Christmas when the festive spirit was most conducive to sharing and enjoying a glass or two. Several chapters however may read like a guide, though this is only because of our experience with terroir, culture, history, appellations, philosophy, winemakers, wine tasting, wine collecting, neuroscience and on being a wine judge. But rest assured, everything is practical and has added to our enjoyment of wine, we hope you will learn from our experiences and mistakes and really hope it will add to your enjoyment too.

Acknowledgements

In general terms I would like to acknowledge every single vigneron, winemaker, tasting guide, brasserie waiter and wine merchant we have ever met where we have experienced nothing but politeness and enthusiasm often tempered with lots of patience. We have such memories of Valerie at Nuiton Beaunoy, Sylvie at La Chablisienne, Richard at Domaine Les Malandes, Fred at Pavillon Gaunoux, and many more.

The whole family of Domaine Michel Rebourgeon in Pommard have become good friends, how often does one get invited into a vigneron's cellars annually to taste from the barrels? With Steve, Delphine and William it happens every year! They have totally embraced us within the "it's not about the wine" concept and we acknowledge how much their friendship means to us.

As a family we also would like to acknowledge the owner and whole staff at Hotel Le Plantagenet in Chinon who look after us so well every time we visit. It's almost as if they know our needs before we ask for anything whether it's room types, dietary needs, restaurants, vineyards to visit or to hire something. Their warmth towards us has permeated a discussion we had recently about where we might buy a holiday home, it wasn't even close with anywhere else, the answer was Chinon!

In writing this book I have needed considerable help of two types. Firstly technical help and I wholeheartedly appreciate and acknowledge all of the help given to me by Danell Nelson, my sommelier friend in Italy. The book cover was designed by her and she created many of the caricatures of myself used in a number of chapters. But above all the chapter, Wine with Art, was a complete collaboration between us as Danell applied her knowledge of art and the aesthetic relationship to wine. When you read that chapter she contributed so much of the insights and interpretation.

Danell is a sommelier living in the South of Italy where she organizes private wine tasting events. She received her certification and training from the Associazione Italiana Sommelier and has a specialized knowledge of Italian wine and culture. She also holds a BA (Hons) in Dance Theatre from Trinity Laban Conservatoire of Music and Dance in London where she had the opportunity to cultivate her love for creativity and the arts. Her wine blog, Vinthroplogy, explores the connection between wine, art, philosophy and culture with topics that range from cubism, to metaphysics, to illustrated wine tasting notes. She also writes articles about wine and paintings for the website www.club-del-vino.com. She is currently working on developing tasting events, workshops and courses for her wine club to continue sharing her passion for wine and the arts and you can see some of her work and contact her here:

- https://vinthropology.wordpress.com/
- https://www.instagram.com/vinthropology/
- https://twitter.com/vinthropology

Finally, and most importantly, I have needed encouragement and patience from my wife of 49 years, Champa, the first woman from Nepal to gain a PhD ..... in ANY subject. She is teetotal too, just like our late son, and has shared all of these wine adventures engaging with the history, the science, the art and the philosophy ...... for her ..... it was never about the wine!

Praise For The Author

*"I have had, what I can only call, the pleasure and fortune of conversing with Dr. B on the question of wine, and he has a certain sincerity and curiosity that speaks not only of wisdom but individual thought. Rather than impose meaning on wine, he is skeptical, rejecting absolutes, generalisations and preconceived notions as adequate descriptions of what wine really "is", while accepting that the mind is nonetheless reflected through it. However often we may disagree, I'm struck by the alluring wisdom in his shedding of what could be superfluous, illusory, or otherwise considered affectation, in order to allow the wine to speak for itself. Paradoxically, this insistence on what wine is **not** has led to creating truly meaningful experiences of what wine has the possibility to offer. It seems that it is this reversion to simplicity which allows one not only to listen but also to reap the benefits of it.*

Dr. B is a retired English man who enjoys traveling with his wife, Dr.C, philosophy and wine, in search of the Epicurean sense of a good life. He is a member of The Wine Century Club and The Wine Society (UK) and has recently been selected as a judge for The People's Choice Wine Awards. Among his many accomplishments he has received a MSc and PhD in analytical chemistry, a BA Hons in psychology, and has run an education charity in Nepal together with his wife.

His exploration of wine and philosophy are intricately connected evolving throughout his life as a relief, a metaphor, a teacher, a mirror, a travel guide, and ultimately a meaningful source of pleasure and reflection."

Danell Nelson, Sommelier, Italy 2020

Dedication

This book is dedicated to our late son Michael who left us in 1997 at the age of 22. He was teetotal all of his life, and yet at the age of 12 walked alongside the vigneron in Meursault and interpreted for us as we were guided through the cellars of Ropiteau Pere et Fils and a wine tasting which included some Aligote. He missed so many of our wine adventures included in this book, but would have joined in all of them without tasting a drop as he totally epitomised that it's not about the wine.

Chapter 1
It's Not About the Wine

"For at the end of the day, what matters is never the wine, it's always the moment; it's always the people." — Olivier Magny, Into Wine: An Invitation to Pleasure

A very long time ago our family decided that any visit to a vineyard or winery should focus on a LOT more than sniffing, slurping and buying a few bottles and which now has influenced the writing of and title of this book. I'm well known for my oft repeated phrase "it's not about the wine", a phrase I borrowed and changed from the disgraced cyclist Lance Armstrong .... "It's not about the bike". In his autobiography Armstrong told of a "journey" to overcome cancer and win numerous Tours de France and so irrespective of performance enhancement via drugs, the phrase is about the time, effort, problems, the science, the ambition, the strategy .... to achieve something remarkable. And so it is with that bottle of wine you are about to taste a sample of. It begins the day a young vine is placed in the soil. Not just any old vine in any old soil, but a specific grape variety best suited to THAT soil, in that position, in that climate. Also remember it was planted by a specific person, someone with a belief and a plan to create a wine of a specific type and following a particular process. The process begins with that planting, but continues as the seasons progress with pruning, tying, feeding, weeding, harvesting, crushing, fermenting, analysing, bottling, storing! Then they open a bottle for you to taste ..... how do you react, what do you say, what do you ask them? Have you done any prior research?

Now, to some of you this may seem a little "over the top", but not if you begin to consider the things I have just mentioned and realise that your pleasure in the tasting can be increased by adding some cognitive input to the sensory. At a basic level it's knowing the grape, the soil and aspect, the ageing whether in stainless steel or oak, and a little of the vineyard/winemaker history, in other words .... some prior knowledge. Your understanding will grow as to why this wine is more acidic than that one, why another has more tannin than the first, whether a biodynamic approach in this field produces a wine of a different taste from the other field using pesticides. Then, there is the wider and deeper comparative knowledge that builds up over time as you visit more vineyards, taste more wines of the same grape but growing in different soils and made by different winemakers, some with pesticides, some organic, some biodynamic. It's not JUST about the wine!

If you are interest in this as a philosophical subject related to wine I can recommend an article presented by philosopher Kent Bach, "What good is knowledge in enjoying the experience of wine?"

Our visits to vineyards are always conducted like this: prior research, taste, ask questions, compare, and as an introduction to this you might be interested in three tastings we conducted across a single day during a family holiday in France in Savennières and Chinon in 2019:

We arrived at Savennières around 11am and parked only a few yards away from the entrance to Domaine du Closel owned and run by Evelyne de Pontbriand. Their most famous vineyard within the whole domaine is Clos du Papillon, a butterfly shaped climat, hence the name. The soil is very shallow here, full of schist, but wines have been made here for generations. The Fief des Vaults is mentioned in 1495 in the Chateau des Vaults archives, with its vineyard, orchard and garden. The chateau was built in the XVII century and remastered in the XIX century. The park with its current design was created around 1850. The property has been in the hands of members of the upper class of Angers and of the prestigious family of Nantes shipowners and later, in the 19th century, the family of Emmanuel de Las Cases, Napoleon's biographer, inherited the estate. Since that day, the Château des Vaults and the vineyards have been managed by the descendants of Las Cases, including Evelyne de Pontbriand the current owner/Manager. Evelyne is from a long line of women winemakers, first started by Marque de Las Cases du Closel. Her niece, Michèle Bazin de Jessey, developed the vineyard and created the company, Les vins Domaine Closel, which she has handed down to her two children one of which is Evelyne. As far as I can work out she is the 5th generation of women winemakers here. The wines here are mostly white, made from the Chenin Blanc grape and all usually long lasting with years to develop to their full potential. The best of them challenge the Grand Cru of Chablis for complexity and ageing potential.

The previous paragraph represents the cognitive aspect of our tasting here, a range of knowledge we have about the wine before we even begin. Our tasting on a hot sunny morning in mid July was managed by Adeline once again who we had met on previous visits. We slurped our way through wines grown on differing soil variants, La Jalousie, Les Caillardieres, and Clos du Papillon, with each increasing in depth of flavour, complexity, length of finish …. and price. Unfortunately, Evelyn the owner was away at a conference in Germany but had left me a present of a voucher for a full tour of the vineyard, the chateau, and a special tasting of different vintages for our next visit. We bought a few cases and sauntered off for lunch, we had more tastings of the same grape in a different district later that afternoon.

Driving back to Chinon after lunch we discussed the wines we had tasted, did they meet our expectations, how did they compare with other Chenin Blanc wines we had tasted in the past, how did they compare with previous tastings in Savennières? Our first tasting of these wines was in 1987, our daughter was almost a teenager (!) but even she has retained those memories, and this is another cognitive element of knowledge I was writing about above, memories of how the same wine has tasted previously. After a couple of hours, late afternoon, we parked at the Pierre & Bertrand Couly vineyard just outside Chinon only a couple of miles away from our hotel. Before you ask, I was the designated driver as I'm better experienced at spitting the wine out!

We have also visited this vineyard before over several years, but it was a first time for our daughter and her husband. The domaine is more famous for their red wines made from Cabernet Franc, and labelled as Chinon plus the makers name, as convention dictates. However they make a white wine too, just one, and from Chenin Blanc the same as the Savennières wines. The different vintages were much lighter and fruitier than those we had tasted in the morning, more like a grassy Sauvignon Blanc. They were OK for my taste, typically good value for a Chenin Blanc to be drunk on a hot summer afternoon in the garden, but not to Sharon and Michael's taste. I bought a case of their young, fresh Chinon Les Blancs Closeaux.

Later that evening we sat outside our ground floor hotel rooms in the hotel garden area with our own very large charcuterie plus cheeses and salad stuff. Time for one more wine and a continued discussion of the Chenin Blanc grape, different styles of it we had tasted earlier, and comparing them with past experiences. THIS is what Kent Bach was writing about in his article "what good is knowledge when tasting wine?". He was really asking about the extent to which "knowledge" adds to the sensory or aesthetic experience of wine tasting. Our family agrees that it DOES add to the overall aesthetic experience but not the sensory; for example you may have noticed that there are no "tasting notes" in this post, we don't get all those fruit salad flavours that some folks get so don't pretend that we do. Have you ever tried describing the taste of a banana ...... it tastes of .... banana, and because of the knowledge from our past experiences we know what Chenin Blanc tastes like from different soil types or countries. This is what adds to our tasting experience and is partly what we spent the evening discussing over a bottle of wine. You might have guessed it was another Chenin Blanc, we'd been given 4 bottles by the hotel owner so naturally one thing led to another as it entered our mouths and brains and the comparison with other Chenin Blancs from France, South Africa, etc began all over again.

My descriptions of the tastings or drinking of wine on

this particular day in France's Loire Valley typify PART of what this book is about, it's content, and it's style. It's not a manual or a reference book; there are plenty of these around written by brilliant wine professionals. It's not a book about specific wines or a specific country, although France will predominantly appear. It IS a book about 50 years of wine drinking infused with travel, philosophy, art, history, with a smattering of science and psychology thrown in. It's also an eclectic collection of personal experiences that I hope will enthuse you to go beyond the immediate sensory pleasure as your lips touch that wonderfully complex liquid in your glass. Remember, it's not about the wine, it's about so much more!

Chapter 2
Early Learning

"The best way to learn about wine is in the drinking."
Alexis Lichine, American wine dealer and writer (1913–1989)

Grandma's ginger wine was the limit of my alcohol experience by the time I reached the age of 16, unsurprising given that I was raised in the industrial belt of West Cumbria with parents and grandparents being of Cornish Methodist mining stock! By the time I was 19, pints of "best" Northern bitter were regularly consumed on Friday and Saturday nights with an introduction to wine being a glass or two of Port at Christmas. But over the next 10 years a number of brilliant experiences opened the door into the world of wine.

It was during university life that I began my wine tasting journey from "wine bluff to wine buff" when I was 22 years old, and now in my 70s I cannot believe how much cheap Spanish and Austrian rotgut I poured down my throat by the time I was 23! Yes, Austrian, if anyone remembers Hirondelle wines? However by the time I was 24 I had also swirled, sniffed and slurped a fair number of classed growth red Bordeaux, some fine Burgundies, and even a Chateau y'Quem, (You might need to Google that!)

via lots of self organised tastings.

Having made ourselves thoroughly ill several times, a small group of us at University of Strathclyde, all postgrads doing PhDs, decided enough was enough. The time had come for some serious research into grapes, countries, bottles, labels, corks, the whole bloody lot, because it sure as hell wasn't "quantity" making us ill since big Frank could down more German lager in a Beerkeller over a weekend than the whole university rugby team! We were all doing PhDs in Chemistry, so tackling this systematically and scientifically was a doddle. An elite club was formed, weekly subscriptions of 2s/6d (12.5p) were paid into an old biscuit tin, and at the end of the month 90% of the money was allocated for a wine tasting of wines purchased from Oddbinns or Peter Dominic wine merchants. The key variables were price, grape, country. At this stage of our young lives we equated cost per bottle with quality so the purchase of 20 bottles or 2 bottles with the allocated cash indicated whether we were genuinely researching something or just getting pissed!

Our research textbook was The Penguin Wine Guide, 1970, and we began by reading up on grape varieties particularly Pinot Noir, Cabernet Sauvignon, Merlot, Cabernet Franc, Chardonnay, Aligote, Sauvignon Blanc, Chenin Blanc, Riesling, Gewurtztraminer. This led us to unravel the mystery of why one wine could be Chardonnay, Chablis, France, another be Chardonnay, Chablis, Chile, yet another be Chardonnay, Chablis, USA! You see in those days, Chablis was marketed as a TYPE of wine rather than as being from a specific village/region of France. The same was true as we demystified Chilean

Burgundy and Australian Burgundy from the REAL Burgundy with all three being made with Pinot Noir but only one actually being from the REAL region of Burgundy in France.

I think you're getting the message here, with our student wine tastings we travelled the world in a bottle on the last Saturday evening of every month for 3 years. Some evenings involved a single grape from a few countries, or from one country but different years/vintages. Some evenings we had just ONE bottle of something with our whole months money such as a Gevrey Chambertin, a Haut Brion or an Y'Quem. The learning was astronomic, the fun we had was awesome, and because of it today any of us can walk into a vigneron's cellar in Burgundy for example, look at his wine tasting list, choose three to taste, then purchase the best value for money either for drinking young or laying down. And certainly today as I swirl, sniff, slurp that first sample of wine, my synapses recognise the grape and its key elements of tannin, acidity, fruit, and finish, but most of all they bring forth mental images of those Saturday nights in Glasgow as big Frank said "bloody hell that's good, have we only got one bottle!" He's learning!

After leaving university in 1974 we bought our first house in N. Wales just over the border from Chester and soon made friends with other professional couples working at the local steelworks. And .... surprise surprise they all had an interest in wine, so before long another "club" was formed with 5 couples agreeing to meet regularly and share our wine, food, and experiences. Our general strategy was to meet on the last Saturday evening of each month at one couples house who would lay on a dinner with every couple bringing along a particular bottle of wine they wanted to share and discuss. From a personal viewpoint this was my "claret period" and my main suppliers were from Tanners in Shrewsbury by post, as well as visiting the rather posh wine merchants Quellyn Roberts and Duttons in Chester, as well as Willoughbys in Altrincham. Quellyn Roberts traded as a wine merchant in a 13th century medieval cellar in Watergate Street for 150 years until closure in 2006. It was a most unique experience descending from street level into the shop front, then deeper still to explore the wines on sale which undoubtedly prepared me for walking through subsequent cellars in France. For the last few years however the building has been leased by Corks Out, a wine merchant and wine bar with a twist. They have what I call a Wine Juke Box where you insert money, in the form of a prepaid card, then select your wine and volume you require before dispensing. These systems are becoming quite popular and are an excellent way to sample small .... or large amounts of a wine without buying a full glass or a whole bottle. I believe the general terminology for places like this is an Enoteca.

Anyway, back to my claret period and here's a few examples bought from these merchants with vintage, year of purchase and price at the time:

- Chateau Chasse Spleen 1976, (1986, £8.99)
- Chateau Malescot St Exupery 1982, (1987, £11.99)
- Chateau Cos Labory, 1982, (1987, £8.50)
- Chateau d'Angludet, 1984, (1989, £6.00)

Our first ever family tasting and visit to a winemaker in France was in the village of Meursault, it was 1987 over the weekend of their wine festival during July. It was at the premises of Domaine Ropiteau, no longer owned by Ropiteau, but still in a good position in the centre of the village.

We haven't tasted their wines since 1987 though we have visited the village several times. On this occasion we were led through the cellars by an elderly gentleman who spoke only French, was extremely polite, and explained things slowly to our young son who had French as one of his subjects at school. Poor Michael was only 12 years old and stoically did his best as my wife, younger daughter and I tried hard not to laugh. We bought three bottles of Aligote, the "other" white grape permitted to be grown in Burgundy which was much more prevalent across vineyards than it is today. On reflection this was a great experience for all 4 of us, we were nervous having heard so much about the aloofness of French winemakers which on this particular day didn't materialise, and it gave us confidence for more visits on that same holiday over the next couple of weeks. In reality, visiting a French wine village gives multiple opportunities for wine tasting and all things related to wine travel. Meet the winemakers, feel their passion, experience the culture, try the local foods often cooked in wine, and maybe buy a bottle or two to take home. Meursault fits the bill on all of these things.

Anyway, after our overnight stop in Meursault, we were "luxury camping" with Eurocamp, we headed off to The Camargue in deepest southern France on the Mediterranean. We were staying at Grau du Roi, a place we were to return to many, many times. In essence, wine was everywhere, Muscats from Lunel, Frontignan and Beaume de Venise, Picpoul de Pinet around Bouzigues as we slurped oysters and gorged on Moules-Frites, plus Cote Rotie and Hermitage with whatever was on the barbecue ...... legs of lamb or tuna steaks as big as car wheels! The children played with new friends from Holland and Belgium as we cooked and steadily sank into an alcoholic stupor! Unbelievable, all of these wines not only available in supermarkets but at unbelievable prices too.

At the weekend, the first weekend in August 1987, we decided to visit the village of Chateauneuf du Pape. En route we had a short stop at the Tavel Wine Cooperative where we discovered the high alcohol deeply coloured Rose wine the village is famous for, then onwards to one of the most wine-famous villages in France, Chateauneuf du Pape. We had driven north for an hour away from our coastal camp site at Grau du Roi on the French Mediterranean in the searing heat to visit this famed wine village for their annual Fete de la Veraison. Our two children were 12 & 10 years old and were looking forward to the day out, because they knew "it wasn't about the wine" ..... as you will see!

We turned off the A9 autoroute and onto the D17 for a few miles before reaching the outskirts of the village .... to find the road blocked by large wooden barriers stretched between wooden barrels and manned by ..... armed soldiers! Good grief, what's going on? One soldier casually walked up to our car and said ..... in a broad Scottish accent "Hello folks, you here for the wine!" No, it wasn't a pantomime soldier, he was part of the French Foreign Legion who just happened to be manning barriers to keep the whole village pedestrianised for the festival. We were directed to the outskirts of the village to park our car amongst the vines, and it was our first sight of the remarkable terroir here where vines grow amongst large cobble stones known as galets which retain the suns heat keeping the roots cool during the day and warm at night.

We walked a few hundred yards up a narrow road lined with vines and into the village centre where we were transported into a medieval wonderland. Knights on foot and horseback, monks, a pope, archers, jugglers, fire-eaters, musicians .... initially it felt like everyone was in medieval costume, except us. The kids were naturally very excited by this and ran off to explore while Champa and I started to explore the lines of street stalls .... cheeses, hams, breads, roasting chickens, pottery, paintings and of course wines, all free to taste. I also noticed however that most people were wandering around with a typical Chateauneuf wine glass in hand FULL of dark red-purple wine ..... what the heck! At this point my daughter ran up to us and said "Dad come quick, there's wine coming out of the fountain!". In fact a large barrel was suspended in the branches of a very old tree alongside the fountain in the centre of the village, a pipe led from the tree down to the fountain ending in a tap ..... help yourself! Nowadays they do it differently with large barrels of wine on a wooden cart pulled along by a couple of dray horses.

Across the day (and whole weekend) there were archery contests, jousting, sword fights, falconry, a medieval wedding (for two unlucky tourists), and processions through the village every hour. Wine of course was everywhere, not only on street stalls of winemakers from the surrounding area, but village winemakers had opened their doors in the Main Street for a never ending line of tasting after tasting.

Chateauneuf du Pape is a "heavy" wine with up to 13 red grapes permitted in a blend chosen by the winemaker, but the primary grape in this mix is always the Syrah, which may be better known to most New World wine drinkers as Shiraz. It's a warming port-like wine, high in alcohol and full of Mediterranean sunshine, a long keeper as it mellows into a liquid bursting with flavour and begging to be paired with roast beef or game such as venison, pheasant or hare and wild boar. And finally, why is this festival called Fete du Veraison? Well, Veraison is the moment in the vineyards when a red grape begins to ripen from green to red, NOT an all-in-one transformation across the grape surface, but as a SINGLE red spot which slowly begins to spread across the grape from that single spot. So now you know just how crazy the French winemakers are, celebrating for hundreds of years that magical moment in time when the journey from unripe sour grape to a beautiful living liquid begins.

Fete de L'Escargot, (Dordogne), Fete de La Moule (Boulogne), Fete de L'Huitre (Arachon) are all annual festivals in France symbolic of their culture and gastronomy involving snails, mussels and oysters respectively. There are many others across the summer months "honouring" French cheese and ..... strangely ...... paella in the Languedoc. Then of course there are the quite stupendous wine festivals celebrating centuries of winemaking in regions across the whole country, and I have had a lot of fun visiting such occasions at Ribeauville in the Alsace region, at Bourgueil in the Loire Valley, as well as at Chateauneuf du Pape in the Rhône. Such memories, tasting maybe 70 wines over two days in Ribeauville, sharing a VERY large glass of Cabernet Franc with Bacchus on his chariot paraded around the town of Bourgueil. But that first visit to a festival in 1987 opened our eyes to the depth of culture that surrounds winemaking in Europe, and we now have a host of memories from several visits to Chateauneuf du Pape for their medieval festival held annually over that first weekend in August.

On the way home from the South of France we stopped off for a couple of nights at Saumur in the Loire Valley. Now brimming with confidence we asked at the campsite for the best local winemaker to visit and without any hesitation the campsite manager handed us a leaflet about Gratien & Meyer who specialised in sparkling wines, Cremant de Loire. So, the next day, off we went to learn about Saumur's answer to Champagne ..... and learned a heck of a lot more about Mr Gratien and Mr Meyer historically and culturally. We've been back there many times since 1987 and ..... it's not about the wine ..... which I'll describe in a later chapter!

So, for those of you who were expecting technical tips

and guidance on wine and tasting I hope my initial stories have inspired you. As you can see, there is no shortcut to "wine fitness", it requires dedication, commitment, effort and practice. You don't get fit by reading a book about fitness! But experience, curiosity and prior knowledge plus a wine tasting approach is essential. Reading, tasting and travelling to vineyards and wine regions is an absolute must. You should experiment too, conduct your own wine tasting of some choices from a local supermarket, go to a good local wine merchant and get to know them for advice, learn about horizontal and vertical wine tastings so you don't just randomly try wines. Keep a log of your tastings, maybe have your own blog. But, most of all have fun, make your wine tastings a social event.

Chapter 3
Wine And Travel Connections

Although the core subject of this book is wine, it should be obvious from the first chapter that there are strong connections with travel. But there are also strong connections with history and philosophy, as well as chemistry and neuroscience, also not forgetting culture and food. Some of these connections and our experiences of them will be explored in later chapters, but it's time now to give some firm grounding in the travel aspect of wine ..... and as the book title suggests ..... it's not about the wine!

My wife Champa (Dr C as she is affectionately known) and I have travelled extensively over the past 35 years and taken in Nepal (her birthplace), Thailand, China, Venezuela, USA, and lots of European countries either directly for long weekends or holidays, or as part of cruise holidays several times in the Mediterranean or North Sea. On reflection "wine related exploration" has figured heavily everywhere except, much to our regret, in China and USA which were both package holidays with tight group schedules. We still drank plenty of wine though! So, before more detailed chapters to highlight some extensive wine and travel experiences in France, here's a few examples of the wine and travel connection in other parts of Europe.

Cruising in Cadiz

The first port of call on most Mediterranean cruises from the U.K. is often Cadiz, the oldest inhabited town of the Western world. Founded by the Phoenicians almost 3000 years ago it was a great trading port which even took them to Cornwall in South West England searching for tin. But walk around the narrow streets of central Cadiz or wander around the beach roads of this peninsula and you just wouldn't know it.

I looked in vain for signs of ancient history but apart from a few crumbling walls of a Roman Amphitheater behind locked gates ..... nothing! No signs of Greeks, Romans, Visigoths or Moors, although in the latter case you could argue for a bit of architecture. But most is from the 18th Century when Cadiz was a wealthier city than London, for 30 years anyway until Nelson and his flcet let rip because the French fleet under Admiral Villeneuve was cowering in Cadiz harbour. Big mistake coming out to Trafalgar Villeneuve old chap, should've stayed in port!

I left the cruise liner Oriana around 10am to a wonderful sky with morning light shining off the rooftops and the top of the relatively modern cathedral. It only takes 10 minutes from the port to walk around part of the waterfront and then inland to the cathedral square. The cathedral was closed and I have no idea why, so I went into a small bar to wait for a while and ordered a Manzanilla. The waiter brought me a cup of tea! I soon discovered that manzanilla is Spanish for chamomile so naturally he brought me a cup of herbal tea but after a few laughs eventually I got the Manzanilla dry sherry I'd asked for.

Fantastico!

I gave up on the cathedral and walked a few streets to the Mercado, the main indoor market which contained the best, cleanest, most artistic variety of fish and seafood I have seen anywhere in the world. Although the fish stalls were brilliant, colourful and artistic, they weren't what I was looking for. I was on a mission to find a tapas bar serving the three types of Spanish ham. I wandered back towards the ship before stopping in a restaurant in a large plaza near the cruise port and ordered a plate of Jamón Iberico, with a glass of Manzanilla of course.

I sat there in the sunshine for about an hour with my iPhone researching the background to this dry Manzanilla sherry (Jerez) I was sipping. It was a perfect accompaniment to my Jamón Iberico and I discovered that it is produced in the Cádiz province/area from 4 specific grapes; Palomino, Pedro Ximénez, Moscatel de Grano Menudo, and Moscatel de Alejandría.

It was now that myself and other passengers from the ship, started to be besieged by a combination of street performers and beggars around our tables, though at times it was hard to tell the difference! An accordionist followed by a guitarist, then a flamenco dancer, a clarinetist, and another guitarist. None played for more than 5 minutes but all of them rapidly walked between the cafe tables with a hat or a box expecting payment. The beggars were incessant too asking for money for food, money for the bus, or for their children. One man put a plastic covered card on each table which read "I have three children to feed please help me". I took out my phone to photograph it but he snatched it up when he saw me doing it. But this led to some fun as I realised that none of them wanted their photographs taking ...... so fun for the next 30 min was holding up the phone each time a beggar approached and watching them move on ..... pronto!

Another Manzanilla and it was time to return to the ship, but the point of this tale is a simple moral or mantra when travelling .... "think local, drink local,"and this will reoccur constantly across this book.

Buddha walked into a wine bar ......

We decided to spend Christmas in Budapest with our daughter and her husband, a city we had all wanted to visit, and going at Christmas would make it extra interesting because of Christmas markets. A British Airways flight from Heathrow took just a couple of hours and we arrived mid afternoon with a pre-booked taxi taking us to our hotel, the Buddha-Bar Hotel near Elisabeth Bridge on the Pest side of the River Danube. We had chosen this hotel for a number of reasons, it's situation on the banks of the Danube, easy access across the Elisabeth Bridge to the Buda District and the castle, it's facilities including the cocktail lounge, brasserie and Asian fusion restaurant, and the really interesting decor and styling throughout the hotel of deep red and black colours with Buddhist icons and Buddha statues everywhere. As

Buddhists, my wife and I loved it! An extra reason for choosing this hotel was that it was on the route of the tourist Big Red Bus, one of those double decker things, often open-air upstairs, that takes you in a circuit around a city seeing the major sites. We've used them before in Rome, Madrid and other large cities and they are great for initial orientation and getting your bearings for the city's main features. And so today after checking in we hopped on one of these and relaxed as we followed the route on a large tourist map we'd been given and listened to highlights via the bus earphones system. It took just over an hour, Buda Castle, The Danube, the parliament building, the UNESCO site of Heroes Square and so much more.

We had decided to have an early dinner in the hotel restaurant and took our seats at 7pm looking forward to some Asian Fusion. The wine waiter/sommelier arrived and asked us if we would like something to drink .... and the fun began! "Yes" I said, "we'll be sticking to wine mostly, do you have some furmint"? There was a quick and faint look of surprise on his face before his composure reasserted itself and a conversation began about how we knew about furmint and had we had it before. In fact none of us had tasted furmint before but exploring the indigenous grape varieties of ANY country is top of our list before visiting, and this is what we told him. He said he would be back, and a few minutes later returned with 4 bottles of wine, two were furmint and two were harslevelu, both Hungarian white wines.

He began opening the first and said "please, I would like you to try these before you decide which you like, and welcome to my country"! How about that for a welcome, and all because of a little knowledge about grapes? All 4 wines were brilliant and we decided on one of the furmint to go with our dinner which was outstanding. Now, the wine connection of this trip doesn't end there because two days later it was Christmas Day and we had booked the special lunch in the hotel restaurant, another Asian Fusion affair but this time it was a never ending help yourself buffet of hot and cold food .... and wine. All at a cost of £35 each, a bargain to wine buff foodies like ourselves. We started on the seafood platters for starters and walked over to the wine station area where you could help yourselves to any of the wines opened, naturally there was furmint and harslevelu, plus chardonnay, sauvignon blanc, merlot, malbec etc etc. Our friend the sommelier was there serving and he wished us a Merry Christmas and looked very pleased as we all chose the harslevelu white wine. For our next course it was on to the hot stuff, lamb, beef, chicken all Asian style, and I wandered up to the wine area wondering what to have now. I stood looking at those international red grape varieties and my face must have given away what I was thinking as our new friend said "have you ever tried our Hungarian red kekfrankos sir, I'll go and get you a bottle".

The sacristan's wife

My third and final example of the travel and wine connection in this chapter is of another family Christmas spent in Spain in the Murcia region to the south and with a Mediterranean border. We are members and shareholders in the UKs Holiday Property Bond and had booked a week in a large apartment beginning 21st December for 7 days. It's a beautiful landscaped holiday facility set in the tiny village of Alfaix. Relatively isolated you need a car for the week and this enabled us to visit the coast as well as the city of Almeria where we had some brilliant tapas and wine experiences. We arrived a few days before Christmas and booked ahead for Christmas Day lunch at the Restaurant Miramar in   Bedar village in the inland mountains away from the sea. We had heard about their famous 24 hours slow roasted leg of lamb for two people so booked a couple for the 4 of us. This was the first mistake, portion control was non existent and a single leg of lamb would have served 4! The second mistake was ordering starters!

However if the roasted legs of lamb were the centrepiece of lunch then the wine we ordered was the supporting act that held the meal together. It was a local blend of Tempranillo, Merlot and Cabernet Sauvignon, a splendid red wine made in the nearby city of Almeria and certainly well known to the local Spanish people. We had researched local wines before arriving and here is what we had found on the wine merchants website:

"Tetas de la Sacristana wine belongs to La Bodega Selección de Vinos de Fondón, from the Alpujarra region of Almería, in the municipality of Fondón, located between Sierra Nevada to the north and Sierra de Gádor to the south. The winery is built on top of an old oil mill in Fuente Victoria that the owners transformed to make wine, and currently still preserve the original mill in a museum dedicated to oil. This wine is part of the Protected Geographical Indication "Vinos de la Tierra Laujar-Alpujarra".

It is made with a blend of Tempranillo grapes (which remain 12 months in oak barrels), Merlot and Cabernet Sauvignon (which remain 5 months in French and American oak barrels) in order to preserve its fruity character. It is a clean and brilliant wine, with very balanced aromas between the shades provided by the aging and the good presence of ripe fruit, we find a tasty wine, with a fluid passage, with good intensity, freshness and character. It has been awarded several prizes both nationally, at the Mezquita awards, and internationally at the Bacchus.

Tell this when serving it: The name Tetas de la Sacristana is often criticized for its irreverence and dubious taste, but it really refers to the plots of land where the vineyards are located. There are different versions of the reason for this name, and the most reasonable one is the one that talks about a man many years ago who, when contemplating from a high area the prominent hills where nowadays the vineyards are located (normally covered with snow), quickly came to mind the resemblance with a certain part of the body of the sacristan's wife and the priest's mistress, and that is why the area has been known since those times as Tetas de la Sacristana."

Now, the reaction here wasn't as dramatic as that we received in Budapest, despite the meaning of Tetas, but these people were proud of their mountain lamb, slow roasted in a variety of mountainside herbs and usually served simply with roasted potatoes. For us to have chosen a local wine to accompany it was a mark of respect in their eyes and it wasn't long before we had appreciative glances and smiles from all of the other locals enjoying Christmas Day lunch. Wine can have that effect ... so think local, drink local.

The five essential characteristics of a wine lover

To end this chapter I'd like to end with a paragraph from the Vinography blog of Alder Yarrow in which he describes what he believes are the 5 essential characteristics of a wine lover. *"When I speak to many wine drinkers, they often express a similar sentiment. They tell me that they really enjoy wine, but they don't know much about it. With varying degrees of embarrassment or chagrin, they describe their interest in experiencing more of what wine has to offer, but then go on to cite any number of factors that they see as barriers to their own ideal relationship with wine. How do we actually progress from habit to true love affair? Most people believe what they are missing involves knowledge that could fill several textbooks. Certainly the difference between a true connoisseur and an enthusiastic wine lover involves quite a bit of understanding of wine's complexities. But some things are more important than book learning. Here then, are five essential characteristics of a wine lover that, if embraced, can forever change your relationship to wine."*

Aldo Yarrow, The Five Virtues of A Wine Lover.

1.	Curiosity
2.	Hedonism
3.	Forgiveness
4.	Patience
5.	Camaraderie

Do you agree with them? Because I certainly do and I think that they are clearly revealed in this chapter, so why not head over to Aldo's blog article and see if you match up?

Chapter 4
Fruit Salad Bingo!

"If it looks like a banana, feels like a banana, and tastes
like a banana, then it's a banana!"
(Personal mantra)

I've used this phrase personally so many times I've lost
count. I've irritated sommeliers, wine journalists, wine
bloggers, but never winemakers with it. Mostly I've
uttered it as an irreverent joke, but occasionally in rage
when a "professional" within the wine industry has tried
to coax, steer, or even bully me towards describing the
micro aromas and flavours I was supposed to be
experiencing. Other folks around the table are often
sympathetic to sommeliers however and join in with
calling out "peach, lemon, honey, butter ...." and so on with
what I have since come to describe as Fruit Salad Bingo ......
the more fruits you can name the more you are acclaimed!
One particular occasion stands out, it was another cruise
around the Mediterranean on a ship with an outstanding
wine bar that we visited every day and sampled wines
from their temperature controlled Enoteca system. I
thought it would be fun to attend a "Wine & Food Pairing"
class in mid morning, it wasn't expensive, €10 to taste 6

wines matched with a range of mini nibbles such as prawn, beef, salmon, chicken. There weren't many of us attending which must have been disappointing for the sommelier, only 2 males and a group of 4 ladies arriving together who were obviously part of a group. The sommelier began by asking us to note down then tell him of any wines/grapes we really loved, and those we really hated. Once discussed we began the tasting of each wine as opened with a little dish of the matching food. It worked well, simply showing how the first taste of a wine can be "altered" if the second taste is taken with a complementary food. The supposition of course is that some wines and foods are matches made in heaven, but as I will relate later ..... I don't buy that at all. So leaping forward by 30 mins we arrived at a prawn each and the final glass of white wine; take a sip and record your thoughts/sensations, then bite the prawn sip the wine and note again.

On this occasion the 4 ladies got excited; "ooh that's good, really smooth, I like that, quite sweet ....." and so on. The sommelier now asked us in turn to describe WHAT we had tasted, I was first and said ... "I can taste unoaked Chardonnay which might mean a Burgundy or a New Zealand chardonnay". He replied "yes, but what flavours do you get", so in turn I said "chardonnay"! He was getting irritated, but so was I. After a few more exchanges like this in my own complete exasperation I said "look, if someone blindfolds me and feeds me a banana, a guava, and a mango, to the first I will say it's a bloody banana. I've tasted bananas from all around the world, I know what a bloody banana tastes like!!!" Who the hell thinks "oh, there are notes of pear drops here, etc etc" In reality I know and can distinguish between a ripe banana and a green banana, a Cox's apple and a Bramley apple, and if you stop to think about this for a moment what you are experiencing in your taste is NOT micro elements, but big bold brassy elements such as sweet/dry, ripe/unripe, tart/smooth, acidic/neutral .... many of which CAN be applied to evaluating and appreciating a wine.

So back to those 4 ladies who at the beginning had clearly stated that they didn't like chardonnay, hated it, in fact detested any wine made from chardonnay grapes. The sommelier clearly believed that the ladies really disliked the overoaked chardonnay based wines, particularly from Australia that had swamped the planet at the time that I came to know as "meaty beaty big and bouncy" as a parody of the Who's classic rock album of the early 1970s. What he had given them was a much understated Petit Chablis, unoaked and from Burgundy so as to test their like-dislike threshold. It was a good test, but in my opinion not one that needed any Fruit Salad Bingo! The ladies went away happy and I went to meet my wife who immediately asked "ok, what have you done now!"

Do you have the *curiosity* gene?

Did you know that there are hundreds, yes hundreds of grape varieties out there just waiting for you to taste? From Aligote to Zinfandel each grape will have different aromas and flavours, in turn each one will vary depending on where it was grown, with a Pinot Noir from Burgundy generally tasting different from a New Zealand wine. Even then, a 10 year old Pommard from Domaine Michel Rebourgeon will look, smell and taste different from this years Pommard made by Rebourgeon. "So what" you might say, but if you're a wine lover with the Curiosity gene then knowing a little about the chemistry and neuroscience of wine and wine tasting will expand your enjoyment many times over! Just hang on in there with the next few pages and a little enlightenment should emerge, but you WILL need to try a few things out, practice a little, drink more wine! This is where you discover WHAT gives each grape/wine it's characteristic aroma/taste, and why some people experience a specific aroma/taste and others do NOT.

It's a little confrontational in parts, maybe even cynical of the haughty attitudes of some professional wine writers, sommeliers, and many bloggers who casually bombard us with their tasting notes of "here's what I drank last night"! This section is about differing perceptions in wine appreciation and, to introduce the issue, here's a couple of tasting notes from typical wine magazines:

Chardonnay from Meursault France, Wine Tasting Note:
"Clean, limpid medium yellow with a hint of green, quite rich, a really lovely colour. Touch of new wood on the nose, ripe melony fruit, slightly exotic, stylish and very expressive. Fine, floral, honeysuckle fruit on the palate, with hazelnut overtones, rich and quite buttery, yet good lemony acidity, very elegant but still young. Very good balance, oak and fruit well blended in, an excellent example of grape variety dominated by terroir, great persistence, very good future."
What do you think, does this classy chardonnay from the Burgundy village of Meursault really contain melon, honeysuckle, hazelnuts, butter, lemon? Here's another:

Medoc, Bordeaux France, Wine Tasting Note:

"Deep colour, velvety red, no real sign of ageing, still very youthful and firm berry fruits on the nose, heavily Cabernet in style, blackcurrant leaf, with a cedar wood / cigar box spice coming through, concentrated fragrance followed by rich fruit. Same concentrated, tightly knit fruit on the palate, wonderful ripeness, still showing youthful black currants and blackberries, firm backbone but ripe tannins, superb structure. Overall, a classic Medoc from a top chateau in a great vintage."

This wine is a classic blend of Cabernet Sauvignon, Merlot and Cabernet Franc, but does it also actually contain blackcurrants, cedar wood, blackberries, and blackcurrant leaves?

These two examples of wine tasting notes leave us with two big questions. First, do wines actually contain all of these fruits, flowers and other components as described? Second, does everyone have the ability to sense or detect them by smell or taste? In a more general sense, would you buy either of these wines based on the tasting notes? Or when you have your Friday night bottle of Prosecco with friends, or Sunday afternoon Barolo accompanying the roast lamb, is this how you mentally perceive a wine and describe it to the rest of the family? I know I don't talk like this, but possibly quite disconcertingly I don't even sense, perceive, or experience all those items in that fruit salad bingo listed in the tasting notes. I'm lucky if I even "smell/taste" ONE of those items. So what's going on here, am I suffering from mild forms of Anosmia/Hyposmia or Ageusia/Hypogeusia (a loss of smell or taste) or am I just a wine tasting dunce in the eyes of the experts? (More on these conditions below).

Science or Philosophy?

To my mind (!) however, wine tasting, wine appreciation, wine writing …. is a battle of the senses, and the two armies of science and philosophy! Do our taste buds, nasal passage, neurons and synapses act like a complex Mass Spectrometer, objectively and consistently "detecting, measuring and evaluating" the chemical composition of a wine? Or are these signals whizzing around our "physical brain" filtered, interpreted and perceived by our "subjective mind" which takes the signals from the "Mass Spectrometer" and judges them based on our prior knowledge, past experience, likes/dislikes, mood, environment? Which means of course that what YOU taste in this wine may NOT be what I taste, or heaven forbid, what I taste in this wine TODAY may not be what I taste TOMORROW! Or, and it gets worse, what an EXPERT (!) tells me I should taste in this wine and the food it should pair with just doesn't work for me. And that last point is the crux of it and should stop you from thinking, "hells bells who cares, I know what I like, a wine is a wine and so long as it's cheap and cheerful" because an awful lot of wine is bought and poured away based on the sensory perceptions of professional wine tasters and writers.

So let's debunk some of this with a bit of objective science. Of course these fruits and flowers are NOT present in wines, but Esters, Pyrazines, Terpenes, Thiols are! These are some of the main chemical compounds found in wine that give the wine certain aromas that ARE ALSO FOUND in many fruits, flowers, herbs and spices. So, Butyl Acetate and Propyl Acetate are found in red apples and pears respectively, the difference between these two Esters being a single Carbon atom and three Hydrogen atoms; Next example, 2-methoxy-3-isobutylpyrazine is the chemical found in green peppers and responsible for the characteristic odour and it has an incredibly low odour threshold, meaning that its smell can be detected below the part per trillion level; another example, 4-thio-4-methylpentan-2-one is the chemical giving blackcurrant its particular odour, also with quite a low odour threshold but not as low as pyrazines.

The significance here is that Esters are found in wines made from Chardonnay, Pyrazines in Sauvignon Blanc, and Thiols in Cabernet Sauvignon and Merlot based wines. Our brains detect SOME of these chemical compounds and we think for example … "Green Pepper …. kerching!" But of course we should be thinking "I've got 2- methoxy-3-isobutylpyrazine here ….. anybody else got that too?". These compounds are NOT the fruit etc actually in the wine, but compounds synthesised from and during the winemaking process, especially the fermentation phase when natural yeasts are converting sugars into alcohol, or to keep this theme going … converting the fructose and glucose from the grapes into ethanol! And, as mentioned above, some have very very low detection thresholds … below one part per trillion (ppt) which some of us definitely do NOT detect because we just don't have the right equipment! So it comes back to personal perception as to whether I or you get the same aromas and flavours as whoever wrote those wine tasting notes with a fruit salad bingo section. And if having the right equipment wasn't bad enough there's the issue of our own psychology and philosophy as well as our prior knowledge and experience to take into account too.

Sources of aroma in wines

For those of you who haven't fallen asleep or skipped this section with too much detail let me reveal that there are THREE types or sources of aroma/taste in that glass of wine you are drinking. Some come directly from the grape itself …. "naturally" you might say! But others arise from chemical reactions taking place during fermentation…. and once again, you might say "so what"! And then there is the third type of aroma resulting from the breakdown of these chemicals as the wine ages in the bottle over time.

1. Varietal Aromas: Smells associated with the grape variety or blend of grapes.
2. Fermentation Aromas: Flavours associated with chemical reactions during fermentation as yeasts react with sugars.
3. Ageing Bouquets: Aromas derived from maturing wines in the bottle as chemical compounds break down with time, temperature, and oxygen.

Hopefully by now you're getting it …. if you can learn how to identify these three types of aroma just think how much MORE enjoyable your wine tasting and visits to vineyards might be? Here's a very useful article by Andrea Buffa over at Wine Folly to help you "deep dive" if you want a greater level of information.

I promised above to return to the Anosmia and Ageusia factors in wine appreciation. The first is the inability to perceive odour. A related term, hyposmia, refers to a decreased ability to smell whereas some people may be anosmic for one particular odour! Ageusia is the loss of taste functions of the tongue, particularly the inability to detect sweetness, sourness, bitterness, saltiness, and umami, with hypogusia being partial loss. Of course these five flavour categories are exactly those quoted in many wine tasting notes and here is a scientific explanation as to why some of us "get them" and others don't:

Avery Gilbert (Avery Gilbert, What the Nose Knows: The Science of Scent in Everyday Life (Crown, New York; 2008), pp.233–34.) stated that more than 20 particular anosmias were known with each one affecting up to 75 percent of the US population, and that this was only a small proportion of such variation in smell perception. A classic example of a wine-related specific anosmia is for rotundone, a chemical found in the oils of black pepper. So for some of you who have ever smelled pepper in your Syrah/Shiraz you now know that it's rotundone. But if you don't get that aroma don't despair, because researchers at the Australian Wine Research Institute have found that 20 percent of us have a specific anosmia for rotundone. My wife is in this category and has no idea what people are talking about when they say Shiraz is peppery. A research paper on this work is here from the Australian Wine Research Institute

Tell it like it is!
So, enough of science and philosophy ….. where the heck are we?
Well, all I can state here are personal views, opinions, thoughts and feelings. Here goes:

- I personally find tasting notes written by professional wine journalists a complete waste of time as I don't buy ANY wine based on the label or the fruit salad bingo descriptions!

- The vast majority of bloggers bore most of us rigid with their "here's what I drank last night and here's my super tasting notes". Often not telling us where they bought it from and how much it cost.
- One mans meat is another mans poison, so you like a Shiraz with your steak, I like a Pinot Noir, and ...... my daughter prefers a Chablis with hers .... what's the point of food matching advice.
- Try reading Tim Hanni's book on wine and food matching and you'll NEVER recommend ANY wine again!
- Try reading about Anosmia and Ageusia generally, then specifically about wine tasting, and start to understand the angst of us poor sods who have no idea what kiwi, guava, mango, or any berry you care to mention actually taste like!
- The best wine notes tell you about the vineyard, the terroir, the balance of the wine, and where it might fit in the spectrum of wines of that grape, vintage, style.
- Tell me about acidity, tannin, minerality, fruitiness, ageing potential, and that's all ...... just as every winemaker I have ever met in France does.
- If you're trying to learn more about wine and understand more, have confidence, have faith in your OWN tastes. You know what you like, just experiment a bit, same grape different regions or countries, or different grape around the world, explore a whole country, don't let anybody tell you what you SHOULD experience or taste. It's YOUR

gizmos the aroma and taste is passing through on their way to your brain, there may be some rotundone or pyrazines…. but who cares….. do you LIKE it.

- If you're a wine professional…. before you write those notes or give advice ….. think about your customer!

"We cannot explain an orange to someone who has never tasted one. No matter how well we describe it, we cannot give someone else the direct experience. He has to taste it for himself."
Thich Nhat Hanh (The Buddha's Teaching)

Chapter 5
Not All Winemakers Are Equal

When travelling around Europe, especially France, it is very handy to understand the difference between the key types of winemaker and there are three that are always in my mind when visiting familiar or new wine regions. Vigneron, Negociant and Cooperative are all elements of wine terminology that can confuse but are simple to demystify. In fact knowledge of each is often vital to finding the best tasting and buying opportunities because each is a different type of wine producer. You will find this section handy as we describe our travels in subsequent chapters.

Vigneron

Vigneron; a person who cultivates a vineyard for winemaking and often makes the wine themselves. This is our favourite type of place to visit where often a whole family are involved in every activity in getting their wine into your glass. Their knowledge and experience is colossal, often having been handed down through several generations. An example would be *"Domaine Michel Rebourgeon"* in Pommard, a small producer, who grow the grapes, ferment the wine, bottle it, cellar it, sell it. We will relate many of our experiences with them in the Burgundy chapters.

Wine Negociants

Negociant: A wine merchant who buys grapes from other growers to make a wine under their own name, not the growers name. I'm not a big fan of LARGE negociants, but they have a place in wine tourism especially if you want to visit cellars, have guided tours, and are seeking labelled wines you recognise. I quite like Patriarche Pere et Fils in Beaune who fit the bill perfectly, but there's another important feature of visiting these large negociants which may be a downside for some...... they are quite impersonal. By this I mean that they are usually dealing with large groups, you are led around by someone who is a "staff member" rather than a winemaker of family member, or on the other hand in some places your tour is self guided. Patriarch cellar visits are self guided which suits us down to the ground as we can go at our own pace.

Wine Cooperatives

Cooperative; a group of vineyard owners who pool their grapes to make wines collectively and market them under the cooperative brand. When visiting a new wine region or area the first thing I do is to look for a local wine cooperative. Often you will find this type of winemaker well represented in the Decanter World Wine Awards, they always represent excellent value, have good quality control, provide free tastings of ALL their wines and have enthusiastic and friendly staff. Nuiton Beaunoy in Beaune are my favourite in all of France, I always get fantastic service from Valerie, they have a full range of wines from basic varietal up to Grand Cru, and are most reasonably priced. To be balanced I also like the Cooperatives Chablisienne (Burgundy), Cave de Buxy (Burgundy), Cave de Ribeauville (Alsace) and Cave de Turckheim (Alsace) too.

Chapter 6
2015, Loire Valley, Chinon

It had been almost 25 years since we had visited Chinon in the Loire Valley and returning in 2015 was a spur of the moment decision. It was also one that changed our outlook on visiting wine regions in Europe and catalysed a completely different focus on future travels. We had been staying with friends at their holiday home near Lorient in Brittany for a few days, and being retired we had no fixed schedule or ferry booked to return home. A few taps on the Booking.com app on my iPhone and we had booked 5 nights at the the Hotel Le Plantagenet in Chinon, Place Jeanne d'Arc, a 3 star hotel with 5 star staff, service and breakfasts, situated on one side of the Place, which has 100+ free parking slots, with the River Vienne on the other side. The only thing to know about parking is to move your car out of the Place the night before any market day if you don't want it towed away! Also, rather than a day by day account of our stay here I'll just give you the wine related highlights which really did pave the way for further trips AND this book.

A horizontal tasting!

Breakfast was the complete cold table so often found in most French hotels with cereals, cheeses, hams, smoked salmon, boiled eggs, cornichons, fruit salad, fresh fruit, three types of bread, orange juice, apple juice and of course a continuous flow of tea and coffee. All "self serve" and as many times as you like. This was our breakfast after a good nights sleep hastened by a few glasses of Cabernet Franc in the hotel which admittedly tasted a little austere. We emerged into a glorious blue sky day and had a walk around the ancient town centre to orientate ourselves before taking the lift from the central car park up to the chateau area. Chateau Chinon is somewhere we hadn't visited since the late 1980s with our children, but there was no chance of nostalgia this morning .... we were on a mission. Cave des Silene is situated above the town adjacent to the Chateau and comprises a wine bar, a wine shop, and a restaurant serving mostly cold platters. It was 11.30am so just time for a special wine tasting before lunch on their sunny patio looking across to Chateau Chinon. The Cave des Silene is owned by the same company and family who also have owned Domaine Charles Joguet since Charles retired, the Genet family, and here you will find not only the wines of Domaine Joguet but also the best wines from the length of the Loire including Savennieres, Sancerre and Pouilly Fume. I had done a little research about the best wine producers around Chinon, all making great wines from the Cabernet Franc grape or Chenin Blanc, and the predominant name that kept cropping up was Charles Joguet. Here's a clip from the Kermit Lynch website about Monsieur Joguet:

"The wines of Chinon have long been celebrated. French humanist and native son, François Rabelais, sang their praises as far back as the sixteenth century. However, the distinction with which the appellation is regarded today is due in part to the legacy left by a more contemporary icon: Charles Joguet. This young painter and sculptor abandoned a budding art career to assume direction of the family domaine in 1957. He soon began to question the common practice of selling grapes to negociants, as his own family had done for years. The Joguets owned prime vineyard land in between the Loire and Vienne Rivers, with some of their finest found on the left bank of the Vienne, just outside Chinon, in Sazilly. These very lieux-dits had been recognized for their character and defined before the Renaissance — some even date back to the Middle Ages. Variations in the soils of these alluvial plains were substantial enough to realize that he was sitting on what would be considered in other regions as premier cru and grand cru vineyards. To sell the grapes off or to vinify these individualized plots together would have been madness. Separate terroirs, he believed, necessitate separate vinifications. Over the course of his tenure, Charles took the risks necessary to master the single-vineyard bottling with an artistry that A.O.C. Chinon had never before seen. In so doing, he realised the true potential of the land".

We were welcomed by a pleasant young man who spoke excellent English …….. with a slight Newcastle accent! He was French but had spent a couple of years working as a wine waiter in …… Newcastle! I told him I was very interested in Joguet wines and would like to be "educated" about them. He asked me a few questions about my understanding of terroir, vinification and my personal collection and then chose 4 different wines from different "fields" (terroir) but all of the SAME year, 2011. What followed was undoubtedly a masterclass, this young man knew his stuff in the widest sense, but he had very detailed knowledge about the terroir within which each of these vines had been grown. All were Cabernet Franc, but all were labelled according to their "appellation" within the French classification system, in turn based on a general structure of clay, gravel, limestone, sand and in various combinations, so here are the 4 wines we tasted:

1. Les Petite Roches; made from vines growing on

clayey hills up to a plateau with soil which is slightly calcareous. It is a very light wine, light in colour and with a light fruity taste. Good for chilled sipping outdoors in summer. (€12)

2. Cuvée de la Cure; made from vines planted on clayey-gravelly soils. This was a wine of some substance, good firm tannins which would soften with ageing for a couple of years. Taste of blackcurrant and even a little spice with a long finish. (€14)

3. Les Charmes; the vines are planted in argilo-calcareous soils and are north facing. The wine is vinified in an oak tank then aged for 7 months in oak barrels. Naturally one could taste the oak immediately, but is wasn't overpowering. Still a crisp fruity wine, I would also drink this slightly chilled with a meaty barbecue! (€24)

4. Clos de la Dioterie; made from vines in a monopole historical vineyard with clay-limestone soils, the vines are 90 years old now all of which contribute to a rich complex wine structured for long cellar keeping, probably 12-13 years. This was a cracker, deeper in colour than the others, heavy duty with strong aromas of black fruits and liquorice. (€50)

What you see in the above list is the order in which I tasted them, moving from light to heavy, simple to complex, easy drinking now to long term cellaring, and increasing in price. Remember they were all the same grape, all the same year, so only the terroir was varying. Difficult to describe in words, a horizontal tasting like this is something you have to experience for yourselves. In this case I can say it is one of the best wine tastings I have ever had, and certainly it got me thinking and appreciating a lot more how terroir influences a wine and how we experience its taste. That was 5 years ago and I have carried the lessons from it around with me on all of my vineyard visits across France. Oh, and I still have 5 bottles of the Clos de la Dioterie remaining! Thank you Mr Joguet! And.......... naturally we had a charcuterie platter lunch in the sunshine afterwards looking across the road to Clos de l'Echo, another historic vineyard worth a visit, but not this time.

Wine & philosophy?

Chinon is a very compact town, as far as tourists are concerned, with narrow streets full of interesting shops, cafes, tabacs, restaurants and brasseries, as well as a couple of squares/place all with outdoor seating associated with a wide variety of restaurants. Across the next few days we explored the whole centre and, amongst other things, discovered the brasserie A la Pause Rabelaisienne, the wine bar La Cave Voltaire, a Rue Rabelais, a Rue Voltaire, and a statue of Rabelais staring down at you as you take a lovely simple lunch at Cafe De La Paix. Now, add this to the fact that the logo of Domaine Charles Joguet seen at the Cave des Silene is an image of Rabelais, then something is afoot here Holmes, and it's connected to philosophy! I'll leave this for now because there was a lot of research involved that we used to enhance one of our later visits and describe in a subsequent chapter.

A Royal Abbey

Fontevraud Abbey is one of the great historic places to visit in all of France and if you are visiting this area it's a "must see" place. Situated half way between the wine towns of Chinon and Saumur it was founded in 1101 by Robert d'Arbrissel. Not long after, in 1189, it became a tomb for some of the greatest monarchic aristocracy of France and England. Here you will find the tombs of Henry II of England, Eleanor of Aquitane his wife, and Richard The Lionheart their son. Also buried here is the wife of King John, Richards brother which seemed strange to us, but NOT King John! However "part" of John was buried here but it was stolen at the time of the French Revolution, a mystery I had to unravel by asking one of the curators of the Abbey during our visit! It was a wonderful afternoon visiting here after a lunch at the Hotel La Croix Blanche just a few metres away from the Abbey entrance and we returned to sit outside in the evening sun with cold drinks before returning to Chinon. It had been a memorable visit and it was another factor which featured in our planning for another visit to this region and a chance to explore further. Later that evening we talked with Martine and Tina at our hotel in Chinon, and with the aid of Google and a few maps plotted a longer holiday that would be based in Fontevraud and open up the wine, the history and much more of this beautiful region of France. It would be three years before we returned as we had a lot of Alsace and Burgundy to explore first as you will see in the next few chapters.

Chapter 7
2016, Alsace, Turckheim

Alsace is France's northernmost wine region, sandwiched between the Vosges mountains and the Rhine it has borders with Germany and Switzerland. It has alternated as being part of France and Germany several times over the last 200 years and much of the population is German speaking and village names seem German in origin too. The region has colourful and distinctive architecture, the food is different in nature from the rest of France, and their wine labelling system is different too. Overall a trip into deepest Alsace gives you the impression of being in a country other than France and this was another short trip of just a couple of days en route to Pommard in Burgundy. It was a recce, a chance to get our bearings geographically and to understand the wine culture here.

We had travelled over to France via Eurotunnel and spent the night in the outskirts of Reims which cut the journey to Turckheim in half. The next morning we embarked on the second leg of our journey remembering to spell Turckheim correctly for the satnav because there's a Turkheim in Germany! It's about a 4 hours drive but seemed longer because it was still raining cats and dogs as we entered our hotel, L'Auberge du Brand in the main street of this small town. The hotel is of typical Alsace architecture, colourful, lots of wood outside and inside, minimal parking but it's no problem as there is a large car park outside the town walls with plenty of spaces about 100 metres away. Having checked in and booked a table for dinner that evening we decided that our two main goals would be split between this afternoon and then all day tomorrow. Today we would spend time at the Cave de Turckheim, one of the areas largest wine cooperatives learning as much as we could about grape varieties and the classification system for village wines or grand cru etc. Tomorrow we would visit the larger town of Ribeauville and spend most of the day there.

Cave de Turckheim Cooperative

About 90% of wine produced in Alsace is white, the other 10% being Pinot Noir. The predominant white grapes grown here are Riesling, Gewürztraminer, Pinot Gris, Muscat, Sylvaner, and Pinot Blanc and these were all on offer in the free tasting at the cooperative Cave de Turckheim situated about a mile away from our hotel and on the outskirts of the town. On arrival, the first thing you are likely to notice however is a large storks nest on the cooperative rooftop, a very common sight around here and one that would be repeated on our visit to Ribeauville tomorrow.

Inside, there is a long "tasting bar" with serving staff behind it ready to help you from the long row of chiller units behind them. On the bar are copies of their wine lists, which at first can seem rather intimidating as there may be 10 pages of wines of different grapes, vintages and "fields" referred to in the French system as a climat or a lieu-dit. Hang in there for a sentence or two and you will soon understand the difference. A climat is a piece of land or a specific vineyard site that is defined by its soil and climate features which make up another French winemaking term, terroir. So an example of a Grand Cru climat in Alsace would be Grand Cru Brand. However, many climats have been subdivided over centuries into smaller "parcels" and these parcels have their own local traditional name known as a lieu-dit. And that's it, all you need to know for now, so if you see wines listed under the name of a lieu-dit it just means that it's a local name for a particular piece of land in which the vines have been grown. Of course, the trick is to know which lieu-dits are the "best" because of specific terroir features! So, back to the cooperative itself, the large light and airy room has an area full of cases of wine stacked mostly according to grape variety, an area selling Turckheim and cooperative momentos such as corkscrews, glass cleaning cloths, books and branded wine glasses, and finally an intriguing area with glass cylinders about a metre tall containing the various soil types found across the region such as granite, limestone, marl, schist and more. Occasionally, one of the staff would walk around these with a customer pointing out a particular soil type in which a wine on their list had been cultivated. These people really know their stuff.

I was interested in 3 grape varieties, Riesling, Gewürztraminer and Pinot Gris, and introduced ourselves to one of the ladies behind the bar explaining that we were relatively unknowledgeable about Alsace wines especially related to terroir, but had drunk plenty in our time. I think we tasted 3-4 examples of each grape variety before settling on what we wanted to buy. My first choice was a Vieilles Vignes Riesling 2012, which means grown on old mature vines, and with the typical smell and hint of diesel on the palate. I know, I know, it sounds disgusting but it works and soon fades as other sensations take over. So, if ever you get a hint of such an aroma .... it's an Alsace Riesling. My next choice was a Gewürztraminer Reserve 2013, a brilliantly perfumed wine, once again so characteristic of the grape variety and one of the few wines that can be successfully paired with spicy Asian food, including Chinese food. Third I chose a Pinot Gris, Marnes

& Calcaires 2015, this was a young wine from the previous year which was full bodied, low acidity and almost spicy. The marnes and calcaires labelling refers to the type of soil the vines were grown in, marnes being a geological term for a lime rich type of soil mixed with clay and silt, with calcaires also being limestone but containing fragments of fossilised marine organisms. This had been an excellent tasting, but there was a small surprise to come. I had noticed a 2015 Pinot Noir on their wine list so asked to try it, my grape of choice especially if it's a Burgundy. It was a stunner, deep red, full bodied and with a lot of ageing potential. So, I bought 6 of these at €20, 9 Riesling at €12.50, 6 Gewürztraminer at €12, and 6 Pinot Gris at €22, all loaded into the car and we drove back to the centre of town.

Grand Cru and biodynamics

Having parked the car we walked back to our hotel, and noticed a narrow opening opposite leading through an arch and with a hanging sign saying "Francois Baur". I quickly googled the name on my iPhone and found it was not just a vigneron, but one using biodynamic methods. We just had to go in of course, but after a cup of tea in our hotel room!

Shortly afterwards we entered the tasting room of Domaine Francois Baur and had another one of those types of experience that creates a significant shift in your thinking, perspective, outlook ……. and the next half an hour was to completely change the questions I ask and future conversations with winemakers everywhere.

The tasting room was compact with a small tasting counter that probably only two people could stand beside, with wooden floors and beams that somehow reminded me of an ancient barn where livestock had once been kept. I don't mean that in a disrespectful way because the place was clean and lots of the wood seemed highly polished, in fact the room was really charming and so different from the massive modern tasting rooms which are characteristic of wine cooperatives.

The room was empty, no customers, but within a couple of minutes a charming lady arrived behind the counter and asked the obvious question ...... "degustation"? I answered in French and English and she immediately switched to speaking English, took out a wine list and asked us what most interested us. I told her that we had been to the Turckheim wine cooperative and described the tasting we had experienced before explaining that we were staying at the hotel opposite, had seen their sign, were interested in Grand Cru Brand and intrigued by the biodynamic approach. She began by telling us that the winery was founded in 1741, produced about 8000 cases of wine annually and had been certified as organic in 1998 and as biodynamic in 2001. Clearly you have the impression that there's a great deal of history, culture and sustainable thinking going on here and suddenly once again ...... it's not about the wine, it's much more than that.

We tasted three wines, all Riesling, and all from the Brand grand cru vineyard, a massive area above the village and with mostly granite based soil. The lady told us that the word Brand meant burnt which comes from a legend that one day here a dragon fought with the sun, and that the dragon sought refuge away from the sun in a cave further up the hill. Apparently this is recognised as the driest vineyard in the area.

The three wines were all different however, the first was a Riesling Grand Cru Brand 2011 (€15.90), next was a Riesling Grand Cru Clos de la Treille 2009 (€17.40), and the third was a Riesling Grand Cru Brand, Cuvee Thomas 2011 (€17.40). Each wine was completely different from the others, the Cuvee Thomas being much sweeter than the other two which were quite dry and it therefore was a compulsory purchase for my wife. The Clos de la Treille is a vineyard within a vineyard, a walled off portion of Brand owned solely by the Baur family and therefore classed as a monopole with the ability to be organically or biodynamically farmed without contamination from other parts of the Brand area. It certainly tasted richer and more complex than the Grand Cru Brand and this is what led to a discussion about biodynamic winemaking. Now, you have to remember that this was 5 years ago, I knew next to nothing about this approach and did my best to follow what the lady was telling me. Naturally she was doing her best too, but in her third language, and at times it seemed far fetched but I have since learned otherwise. So imagine that this is what you hear: biodynamic winemaking is organic winemaking "on steroids" metaphorically speaking of course, with no pesticides or insecticides, using natural fertilisers like cow manure, special additions like chamomile, fertiliser planted inside a cows horn to rot, and certain activities such as pruning and feeding all linked to the phases of the moon and the four ancient elements of earth, air, fire, and water! I'll pause there so you can stop laughing or go and have a lie down, but don't give up because I have devoted a whole chapter to this added to the issue and effect of terroir. We bought three bottles of the Cuvee Thomas and 9 each of the other two Rieslings before crossing the street back to our hotel for a nice dinner and a good nights sleep. (You might like to know that as I write this in 2020 we still have 2 of each remaining and maturing well, but its probably time to drink up).

A tourist day in Ribeauville

Our plan for today before we left for Pommard tomorrow was basically to be tourists, no wine tasting or vineyard visits, but certainly an exploration of Ribeauville with a view to coming back for an extended stay. The town is at the northern end of the Route des Vins, a meandering string of wine villages where it is so obvious that the people here take great pride in them with colourful well maintained houses, hanging baskets of flowers everywhere, clean streets and tidy clipped grass verges. We parked at the large parking area just off the D1B near the Ribeauvillé wine cooperative, but we weren't tasting today so saving it for another time. From here it was a short walk into the town centre, though on leaving the car park our eyes were immediately drawn upwards to another large storks nest on top of a circular stone building with a conical shaped tiled roof. Not five minutes later there's a stork walking down from the main street like it owned the place!

Across the roundabout from where we'd parked we saw a sign advertising the Petit Train de Ribeauvillé, one of those things that looks like a train but runs on the road pulling open sided carriages each holding 4 passengers. Usually they take tourists around a town centre and the immediate environs and its often a good way to get your bearings when you are new to a small town. So, it looked like a good idea to start our day off in Ribeauvillé, and it was. The little train took us around and through the town centre, down narrow streets and lanes which were either pedestrianised or one-way traffic so there was no problem of it causing a blockage. Supplied earpieces provided commentary you could set to your own language. Ribeauvillé isn't one of those European cities with large cathedrals and historic castles and buildings, it's just .... pretty! The houses are classed as "pan de bois" style which means half timbered which is self explanatory, and they all have clay tiles which are "beaver tail" shaped, and quite steeply pitched too. Then there is lots of colour to the walls between the timber, mostly shades of yellow and orange. Eventually the train moved out of the town and into the surrounding vineyards and what seemed like tiny hamlets, though they are probably still part of the Ribeauvillé town, before taking us back to the central roundabout where we had begun our interesting journey. It was 11.45 and time to find a lunch spot before the mad rush and all of the shops shut!

A cultural lunch

We didn't fuss about choosing a restaurant, there were so many with outside tables it was mind boggling and they were already starting to fill up so we just looked for two things .... a sign that said tarte flambé or flammekueche plus comfortable seats with shade. We settled ourselves down at a table of the Brasserie de la Poste and ordered a couple of tarte flambé, a small carafe of Gewürztraminer for myself and a coffee for Champa, which often baffles waiters in France who only expect coffee orders at the end of a meal. For those who don't yet know much about the Alsace region of France and it's cuisine culture, if you're seeking out classical French cuisine with artistically arranged foods, a multitude of wine based sauces and portion control then you're in the wrong place! This is the land of hearty meals with meat and veg hanging off the plate, especially chunky hams and sausages, with an attitude towards food like the old days in the North of England where Sunday lunches began with a Yorkshire pudding filled with gravy as big as your plate followed by chunks of roast beef, a mountain of roast spuds and other vegetables on a separate plate! Anyway, there's a bit of history to the tarte flambé which tells us that many years ago the people of Alsace with wood ovens who baked bread daily would put a large flat and thin piece of dough into the oven to check it was at the required temperature before inserting their loaves. Pulling out the thin dough they would eat it as an early morning "snack" during their work. Then apparently during the 1960s when pizzas exploded onto the fast food scene the crafty Alsace folks realised they had their own equivalent and marketed it smeared with creme fraiche instead of cheese and topped with lardons. And so the Tarte Flambee Nature was born!

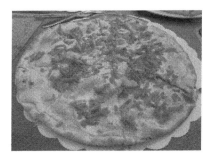

Our drinks arrived swiftly followed by our tartes, and you immediately sensed the long established traditions of

Alsace as my wine glass was the stubby green affair that has been characteristic of this region as long as I can remember.

The wine was well chilled and had the classic spicy perfume of a Gewürztraminer, not a grand cru, just a standard house white and a perfect match for my tarte flambé. We sat in the shade here for over an hour watching and listening to an array of buskers who appeared in sequence along the Grand Rue full of restaurants, and to be honest who were all quite good playing accordions, or violins or clarinets or guitars. Excellent entertainment over an excellent lunch for a few coins each time.

Just wandering

We spent the afternoon just wandering up and down the Grand Rue, in and out of shops, marvelling at the architecture, the wood and metal signs above shops, gazing at the array of breads, pretzels and cakes in the bakeries, and peeking inside the many Winstubs which literally means wine lounge. These originally were places where winemakers sold off their surplus stock to the public in a traditional Alsace setting, but nowadays are restaurants/brasseries/wine bars. As we walked back to the car we both realised that this was definitely a region we would return to and that Ribeauvillé was definitely the place we would stay. We had even selected our hotel and the wine places we would visit, but that wouldn't be for another 18 months, though it would be a cracker of a visit with one VERY special wine!

Chapter 8
2016, Burgundy, Pommard

The Burgundy region of France, Bourgogne, is surely the Mecca of all things wine. Archaeological discoveries prove that the Romans cultivated vines here up to the 2nd Century, then there are the medieval monks who organised viticulture across the whole region with many abbeys, chateaux, vineyards and climats still existing and producing wine to this day. The region stretches from Chablis in the North down to Maconnais in the South. In between we have the Cote de Nuits, Cote de Beaune and Cote Chalonnais, and within each district there are villages synonymous with wine labels that confuse the heck out of many newbies to wine appreciation and collecting. But visit the region just once and I guarantee all will click into place like the reels of a Las Vegas slot machine about to pay out a jackpot! I will write in a separate chapter about some of the history of wine in this region and others, but for now read on as we share some of the fantastic experiences we have had in Burgundy, always involving wine but as our book title asserts, "it's not about the wine".

Imagine I offered you a glass of Pommard or a Meursault, a Volnay or a St Aubin which would you choose? Or do you buy your wine on the basis of red v white, Chardonnay v Sauvignon Blanc, Australia v Chile? All well and good, but that's like going into a butchers shop and asking for "a kilo of red meat please" or, "a kilo of beef please" without getting to the real issue that you want some matured and organic fillet steak of Aberdeen Angus! Buying wine is NO different, especially in France generally and Burgundy specifically. In one part of Burgundy we have the Côte d'Or divided into the Cote de Beaune and the Cote de Nuits. Then in the Cote de Beaune we have lots of tiny villages each with vineyards and entitled to name and label their wines with the village name, and in some cases with even the name of the field/vineyard which may have an entitlement to be called a Premier Cru or a Grand Cru.

If two villages epitomise Burgundy, the Cote de Beaune and red wine, it's Pommard and Volnay. A kilometre apart only as the crow flies, but it might as well be a galaxy apart in terms of the wine differences. Volnay epitomises Elegance, Femininity ..... Pommard exudes Power, Masculinity. These differences are created mostly by slight differences in slope, exposure and surface rock because the grapes of each wine are identical ..... Pinot Noir! On the other hand, walking down the hill into Meursault from Volnay you can't help but start to understand immediately that the wines here are going to be different. Comblanchien Limestone that disappears underground at Nuits St George reappears here and has more clay in the surface mix than its neighbouring Volnay. The slopes are lower and facing a slightly different direction too. Many are quite flat with no slope at all. You are now entering the "white wine villages" of Burgundy .... Meursault, St Aubin, Puligny-Montrachet, ... And here the grape is the

Chardonnay.

Having a wine holiday is about MORE than just drinking wine, or having lots of wine tastings. There are opportunities to discover lots about wine MAKING, the soil or overall terroir of the region, and to meet some of the vigneron themselves. Two we recommend are Domaine Michel Rebourgeon in Pommard, and Domaine Francois Gaunoux in Meursault. The Rebourgeon tasting room is in Pommard, easy to find just inside the village on the right. A small producer with VERY high quality wines reasonably priced, their tastings are free, and likely to be handled by Delphine or her son William, a young up and coming vigneron just out of college. They mostly grow Pinot Noir so have good Pommard and Volnay. The Gaunoux tasting room is on the main road between Meursault and Pommard, near Volnay and called Pavillon Gaunoux. Owned by Claudine and her husband Jean Pierre, their focus is on Chardonnay from high quality fields some of which are monopoles. They produce some reds too notably from premier cru field Les Grand Epenots, at Pommard. Tasting is also free, often run by Fred, and they do great simple lunches too. Both of these vigneron feature strongly in our visits to this region and you will read some details of our tastings and interactions with them in the following sections of this chapter.

It is clearly impossible to completely describe here the variation in culture, style, and charm of the wine villages of Burgundy, but you will be welcomed in all of them by the hard working and friendly vignerons, so why not pay them a visit ...... as we do regularly!

We have visited Burgundy many times but mostly with

overnight stops on our way to somewhere else, always buying wine from a good merchant or wine cooperative, but never really exploring vineyards, vignerons, or villages. In 2015 however, we started to realise just how much we had missed and so organised a "short tour" that would involve staying in the villages of Chablis and Nuits St Georges. We also had visited Chinon in the Loire Valley as an extension to a holiday at a friends home in Brittany. We travelled across to France via Eurotunnel and drove to Chablis for two nights, then to Nuits St George's for three nights, before returning home to England via Brittany Ferries from Caen to Portsmouth. We were really "mapping out" the villages and surrounding areas with an eye to well placed hotels, vineyards to visit, some history and culture of each place, as well as good restaurants and brasseries. It was from this recce that we planned out FOUR superb holidays over the next four years in three great French wine regions and staying in seven different villages for at least a week each time, and sometimes for two weeks. Here's the first during July 2016.

Pommard: July 2016

We had spent 2 nights in Turckheim in the Alsace

region of France on the border with Germany before setting off after breakfast for Pommard. It had been a wet weekend, rain every day, and it didn't bode well for our week in Pommard as the rain hammered down all the way on the A35 as we headed south. It took about 5 hours with a couple of breaks and it was just after 2pm as we came off the motorway at the Beaune interchange. It is just a few miles from here to Pommard on roads we know well, and .... lo and behold the sun came out as 10min later we entered the village and drove down the Grand Rue then to Apartment Charmots in Rue des Charmots. The street and apartment are named after the premier cru vineyard Les Charmots, planted entirely with Pinot Noir vines, which is almost adjacent. A good start!

"Charmot de Pommard offers quiet comfort and luxury in a fully renovated one bedroom apartment located on the ground floor of a 17th century building formerly occupied by a wine merchant. It features limestone floors, oak timbers and stone walls as well as modern appliances and amenities that will make your stay a pleasant one."

We had booked this apartment through Holiday Lettings and the review I left says it all. If you want a luxury apartment in the area for two people, this is the one:
"We have travelled extensively around France and Europe for the past 30 years staying in apartments, cottages, gites and of course hotels and we can say that without exception this is the best standard of property we have ever stayed in! However you want to define quality, this property has it; furnishings, kitchen equipment, cleanliness, even the quality of "extras" like the Occitane hand soaps and shower

gel and the Nespresso coffee capsules. The property is ideally located in the quiet part of Pommard, a stones throw away from vineyards and a few minutes walk from the village centre. During the extremely hot weather during our stay the thick stone walls kept the property very cool. A parking space only a few metres beyond was a blessing for someone not wanting to park a Jag in the narrow streets! What more could you want?"

Once settled in and having unpacked we made the obligatory trip to the nearest large supermarket, a Carrefour at Avenue du General de Gaulle on the south side of Beaune where we stocked up on cheeses, charcuterie, bread, milk and plenty of salad stuff. Naturally a couple of bottles of wine were added, a Pommard, a Volnay and a St Aubin, all from Bouchard Pere et Fils, one of the oldest negociants and merchants in Burgundy, founded in 1731. When you're in a bit of a hurry, think local, know who's who, and grab a couple of bottles! It had been a long drive and on returning to the apartment we ate an early evening salad, had a couple of glasses of Volnay, did a little planning for tomorrow, and fell asleep.

A day in Beaune

The Market

A simple breakfast of cereal, fruit and croissants set us up to leave the apartment at 9am and drive to Beaune, it was market day and something not to be missed especially in wine regions across Europe. We drove into Beaune along the D974 then turned to the right to enter the one-way ring road travelling anti-clockwise until just passing the continuation of the D974 towards Nuits St George. Lots of parking here on your right, even on market days, so no need to risk life and limb by attempting to find a space inside the centre of the town. It's a short walk now under the massive archway into the centre.

Typically every street is packed with stalls and people and unlike a typical British street market this one is colourful and dominated by fresh produce. The array of vegetables and fruits is astounding together with cheeses, hams, bread, patisserie, honey, wines, ciders and you soon realise that almost everything is local, including the stalls selling hats, pottery, tools, and .... those wonderful Poulet de Bresse. There are ready cooked chickens and hams too, roasting on barbecue spits. It's only when you get to the clothing do you realise that this is the only imported stuff on sale! We can only take so much of this, the colours and variety of goods is really overwhelming and it's time to find a cafe or brasserie with a couple of empty seats and sit down with cup of coffee each and a little people watching. It's now that you recognise something else, that so many people here know each other as folks stop to chat, men doff their caps to ladies they know and meet, and there is the ritualistic cheek to cheek kissing welcomes too. This is more than a market, it's a social gathering that has been going on like this for centuries, something we seem to have lost completely across England.

Fortified by our coffee we now set about our own objectives which are Epoisse and Comte cheeses, green beans, new potatoes, mushrooms and a Poulet de Bresse.

"Poulet de Bresse chickens are treated like fine wine. They have an appellation, get to eat real food and strut around the countryside—all regulated by law. The king of chickens is truly a part of French culture. The story of the poulet de Bresse, with its steel blue feet and bright white plumage, begins in 1591 when the bird was first mentioned in the town registers of Bourg-en-Bresse. Henry IV, having stopped off at Bresse following an accident with his carriage, tasted the bird's meat and demanded its inclusion on his courtly menu. Described by the French as 'the fourth gastronomic wonder of the world', the poulet de Bresse comes out on top because of its dense, flavoursome flesh. This is due to the strict government controls imposed in the region of Bourg-en-Bresse, where the chickens are given plenty of space to run around, producing a bird which is high in protein and low in fat." (Quoted from FranceTravelGuide.net)

The Lunch
It only took about 30 mins to find the items we wanted and fill our bags, it was now 11.45am so ...... time to find a lunch table before we got killed in the rush. We avoided the Place Carnot, that was for another day, and scurried down Rue Nicolas Rollin to Dame Tartine restaurant, not a fine dining establishment, but one of those auberge country style restaurants with Prix Fixe menus with 3 course lunches for €10 or sometimes less. What a relief, the place was actually empty, but I kid you not, by 12.10pm every table was taken and the aisles were jammed with

dogs and trolleys! Waiters had to take circuitous detours to get to some of the tables, all done efficiently and without a glower or complaint. We both chose from the fixed lunch menu, 6 escargots for me and oeufs meurette for Champa, followed by steak-frites for myself and a tagliatelle with a mushroom sauce for Champa. No room for desserts, but still a bargain at €10 each. It was now after 2pm and time to move on to the next item on the days plan.

Wine Time.
Back at the car we entered the one way ring road again and continued around until we got back to the same point at which we'd joined it in the morning, and exited taking the same road out of Beaune towards Pommard. About 2 miles down the D974 on the left is a large warehouse looking building but with lots of glass at one corner signed Nuiton Beaunoy.

This is one of the best wine cooperatives in France, first visited by us in 1987, and a big favourite ever since. In fact we've been so often it's hard to separate one visit from another, but I remember this one because of a change in our "buying strategy". Usually we are staying for one night in the area, passing through to the Jura, the

Languedoc, or maybe the Alps, so we have a general idea of the wines that interest us, taste a few then fill the boot of the car! But now we were staying nearby for a whole week and I wanted to "shop around" before buying rather that impulse buying a few bottles. Inside, the tasting area is vast and dominated by a long counter with price lists, a seating area, and shelves neatly organised by wine appellation. It wasn't always like this, 30 years ago inside this same area there was no tasting counter, just 8 large wine barrels stood on end with half a dozen or so opened bottles of wine on each. Staff were floating around to keep the bottles topped up, or to open anything you wanted from the menu. Yes, they would open ANYTHING you wanted whether it was a humble Cote de Beaune or a premier cru Pommard. I believe this was eventually stopped when a fatal accident occurred nearby and one of the cars involved was found to be crammed full of cases of wine from the Cooperative. Very sad if true, but their organisation now is superb, efficient, friendly, knowledgeable, and everyone speaking good English. The only thing I really miss is the sale of wines via the old "en vrac" system, which means "in bulk", and involved wine being dispensed from what looked like a petrol pump gun into your own empty wine bottles they would then cork for you. We used to see locals arriving carrying crates of clean wine bottles into the filling area for their weekly top up, sometimes with several crates one for white wine, one for a simple red, and one for a premier cru something or other. Those were the days!

Within a minute or so of entering, our friend Valerie who works here mid week noticed us and came across to greet us. She is great fun, always remembers that my wife is teetotal and needs somewhere to sit while she and I get engrossed in our deliberations. Today I explained to her that we were staying in Pommard for a whole week and wouldn't buy any wine until the last day when I had "tasted around" the area and could make informed choices. Today I only wanted to taste some of their red wines, no whites at all until we came back in a couple of days time. This was no problem, she gave me a couple of their printed price lists and we began to taste and assess. Remember all reds are Pinot Noir, this is a cooperative so all wines are branded as Nuiton Beaunoy, the range varies from regional blends to village wines to premier and grand cru wines. Valerie knows I am mostly interested in the village wines such as Chorey les Beaune, Pernand Vergelesse, Monthelie for example. These wines are made from vines in the named villages which, despite being of very high quality, cannot command the same prices as the better known Cru wines of Pommard, Volnay, Gevrey-Chambertin and many more. Find the right village, with vines from the right climat/field, from a good vintage, and you will find an absolute bargain at half the price of a wine from a better known village. I have noticed too that each year we visit that there are more of these village wines being made, so new labels pop up meaning more wines to taste, and this time Valerie carefully explained a range of information about each new village, telling me what to expect before I even swirled, sniffed, slurped or spit. They were all of the 2014 or 2015 vintage, so vibrant in their colour of reds and purples, with fresh fruity aromas, well balanced acidity and tannin, and varying length of finish. Very impressive, all of them, but it was the Pernand Vergelesse that really stood out and I gave it a 5 stars grading on my price list. (I use a simple 1-5 star system to rate wines, at the highest level this means "an outstanding wine that will not only mature and age well, but will also appreciate in value, a potential investment.") After tasting half a dozen or so village wines we moved on to the wines of Volnay and Pommard, the two villages next door to each other, but with wines so different. They were really similar to the earlier village wines I tasted, though double the price for straightforward Pommard or Volnay, and treble the price for premier cru versions from single climats. I marked the price list with my notes and said aurevoir to Valerie telling her we'd be back for a tasting of the white wines in a couple of days.

And so we drove back to our apartment well contented with our day, parked the car and then realised just how hot it was with a temperature of 81C, so hurried inside to the surprisingly cool apartment thanks to the really thick stone walls. We set the large fan whirring however and decided on a light salad for evening meal with the days purchases safely tucked away in the large fridge. Our evening planning decided that tomorrow would involve no driving!

A day in the vines

A morning walk

After a fairly hectic day like yesterday we needed something relatively relaxing and had decided on a simple walk between the villages of Pommard and Volnay following the narrow road through the vines. This is a typical road used by the vine workers, good for cycling and walking and with passing places for cars. It's only about 1.5km from Pommard to Volnay and we set off at 10.30 so as to saunter quite slowly and be in good time for lunch. Already there were quite a few cyclists about, usually families of parents with a couple of children mostly on bikes that can be easily hired here in most villages. In fact we are on part of a designated cycle route that stretches for miles and miles navigating between famous wine villages and their vines, all well signposted and with "station areas" where there are large map boards and often toilets and picnic areas too. There were also plenty of workers in the fields above us up the slopes to the right as well as below us to the left. It's very interesting to see here how the slope and aspect affects the grading of the wine from each field/climat irrespective of the owner or winemaker. For example, roughly speaking, on the Pommard side of the boundary high above us to the right is the Les Chanlins Haut climat, which means that any wine made from these vines will be labelled Pommard, Grand Cru Les Chanlins, plus the year and the name of the owner/winemaker/brand. Just below it is Les Rugiens Haut and Les Chanlins Bas, both Premier Cru vines so labelled accordingly. Now lower still but on our left is the

Les Rugiens Bas climat also a Premier Cru, but further below it are the lower graded vines, still Pinot Noir but receiving less sun and possibly in different soil. These features are part of the mystery of "terroir" I will return to in a later chapter.

There is a point at which Pommard officially becomes Volnay, and it's not just some arbitrary line on the ground. It's a point at which "the terroir" changes, especially the soil makeup from clay soils rich in iron to well drained limestone-rich soils and so Pinot Noir wines of quite different character are made. We have often tried to identify exactly the point at which this change occurs but it's not easy unless you know it's where the Les Chanlins Bas climat ends!

So now we are in Volnay and the road name has also changed to be Rue de la Pitures, with a Volnay premier cru climat Pitures Dessus above us to our right and another premier cru climat named Fremiets below to our left. I suppose this has got a bit like "Field Name Bingo" so let me say that it's this sort of knowledge that makes a simple walk much more interesting and it can open up a whole new depth of conversation with the winemaker at a tasting.

The lunch

It's just after 12 noon as we arrive at the centre of the village and wander into the gardens of   Le Cellier Volnaysien, a beautifully combined wine boutique and restaurant, both supporting and serving local wines and local produce lunches and dinners. It was another hot sunny day and Nathalie, the owner, was putting up the umbrellas at each table in the garden already set for lunch.

We had met a year ago when we visited the wine boutique she set up herself in 2013 to add to the restaurant she founded in 1975, on that occasion I tasted 6 different Volnay and bought 6 each of the Henri Delagrange and the Bitouzet Prieur. She greeted us warmly but I don't think she remembered us as we mentioned that we'd prefer to eat in the cellar restaurant which would be much cooler. Stepping inside for the first time can be quite a surprise as you instantly are inside a tunnel-like cellar with a completely curved wall to ceiling interior, which seems to be created just like the dry stone walls of the Cotswolds. Small brick sized light coloured stones, probably of limestone, must have been hammered and chiselled by skilled masons to create this cellar long ago.

Natalie brought us the menu and the wine list and we chose from the fixed lunch menu as we always do in France, a jambon persille as starters, then a chicken breast in a cream sauce, and finally a creme caramel for dessert. I reminded her of our tasting from the previous winter in the wine boutique next door which she did remember because of my car, a large Jaguar XF which they don't see around here very often. So now I asked her if it was possible to have a degustation of 3-4 mini tasting glasses of different wines with the meal from her boutique menu which she readily agreed to and I chose two whites, an Aligote and a Monthelie, and two reds, an Aloxe-Corton and an Auxey-Duresses. She brought the two reds first understandably as they would go well with the jambon persille and as I settled back to enjoy them a group of 5 well dressed French gentlemen arrived and occupied a table close by us, the rest of the cellar being empty. The one clearly in charge obviously knew Natalie well as the first thing she did was to give him a wine list he carefully studied while she was giving everyone else the lunch menus and explaining any specials. By the time she had finished so had the group leader and he pointed to the menu and quietly said something to her about the wine(s) he had chosen. Across the next hour our own food and wines were great but we became completely distracted by the behaviour of these French businessmen. Nothing wrong with it, but it fluctuated between serious business conversation about something engineering and conversation about the four bottles of red wine that arrived at intervals on a signal between the group boss and Natalie. All were different and prompted serious discussion, and it wasn't until they had left the restaurant that I was able to get up and look at the last remaining empty bottle. It wasn't a Volnay, but a Pommard Premier Cru Les Epenots 2010, not even on the restaurant wine list that I estimate would have cost near €200! Anyway, when our own bill arrived Natalie refused to add any payment for my 4 tasting wines even though they were generous portions. We had a conversation about the Aligote I had tasted, quite unusual to see it again on wine lists now with any vines having mostly been replaced with Chardonnay over the years. I asked her to put me a box of 6 aside for tomorrow when I would return with the car and she added the bargain price of €42 for the 6 bottles which might just have bought me a single glass of the Pommard just consumed on the adjacent table!

Fred's Place
As we are leaving the last houses on the outskirts of Volnay returning to Pommard we arrive at the junction with

another vineyard road that descends through the vines to our right to join the busy D973. Here we spot something we hadn't noticed before at the bottom of the hill and it looks like a roadside restaurant, so down we go to explore. Much to our surprise we discover Pavillon Francois Gaunoux, a brasserie and wine boutique/tasting room of Domaine Francois Gaunoux. Now, I know this domaine which is situated in Meursault and with vines planted in some classy climats in Meursault and Pommard especially, but what is THIS place?

We sat outside under a bright red sun shade and ordered two cold drinks from the waiter who came out from the small building to serve us. When he returned I asked him about the place and in excellent English he told us it was one of the two main tasting rooms of the Domaine, the other being in the centre of Beaune, and that everything was now run by Claudine the daughter of Francois. He took me inside and showed me around the place, surprisingly large inside a bit like a Tardis (for Dr Who fans) with a mini brasserie with 6 tables, a second room for wine tasting, and a kitchen at the back. He was really enthusiastic and told us a lot about the Gaunoux family and the energetic Claudine and the fact that he works here three days during the week, as well as weekends at the Gaunoux restaurant in Place Carnot in the centre of Beaune. He was interested to learn about us too and I explained about our wine travels, wine collecting and where we were staying. I made a mental note to revisit here and have a "significant" tasting of the Gaunoux wines, not today as we had a big lunch inside us and a walk back to Pommard in the hot sun. Fred and I parted as if we'd known each other for years, and we now know this as Fred's place and were to have two great tasting events here a year later!

A day trip to Cote Chalonnaise

Today was going to be another scorcher, temperatures in the 90s again so we decided that sitting in the car with the aircon going full blast was the priority of the day! This meant the time was right for our trip to another favourite wine cooperative, the Cave des Vignerons de Buxy. It's less than an hour drive from Pommard via the D973, then the D981 avoiding the large conurbation of Chalon-sur-Saone, and on to their large building at 4-6 Route de Chalon, 71390. We have a particular reason for coming here regarding a particular wine, first tasted many many years ago and still a big favourite with our daughter ...... so we need to buy some!

The cooperative was formed in 1931 and currently has over 120 member vignerons who pool their grapes to make high quality chardonnay based wines under the cooperative brand. Combined, they are the largest producer in the Cote Chalonnaise and account for above 66% of the wines of the Montagny appellation. They are renowned for their Montagny Premier Cru, so no basic chardonnay wines for our daughter! There's a good description of their operation and approach on The Wine Society website and I have placed a link to it in the References & Links section, and you will find a link to the cooperative website there too.

We parked in their large parking area at the front of the building and hurried inside to escape the heat and into a large, airy and air conditioned environment divided into two main areas. The first is a very large tasting room with a circular tasting bar in the middle of which there are serving staff, with the room surrounded on the walls with shelf after shelf of their bottles of wine, red, white and cremant/ sparkling. The second large room is virtually a warehouse stacked with cases of each wine on pallets ready for pickup and placing on a flatbed trolley when you have made your choices and are ready for checkout. I had never tasted any of their reds before so tried a couple while attempting to keep the earlier days tasting of reds at the Nuiton Beaunoy Cooperative in mind, before moving on to the whites of Montagny and then some sparkling Cremant de Bourgogne. As usual the staff in these cooperatives are always a delight, they serve you with great skill and knowledge of each wine and also clearly have great pride in their cooperative. There were two wines that really impressed me, firstly a Montagny Premier Cru, Les Chaniots 2015 and so I bought 6 each for daughter and self, and secondly a Buissonier, Cremant de Bourgogne Demi Sec, also buying 6 each for self and daughter. Both wines got 4 stars on my ranking system and you might be surprised at the price; the Buissonier was only €6.95 and the Montagny Premier Cru stunning value at €9.80! We drove back to Pommard well pleased with ourselves and spent the afternoon cooking a large pan of Coq au Vin using the Poulet de Bresse from the Beaune market and some of the wine bought at the Carrefour hypermarket on arrival day. No cooking notes supplied here except to say we are BIG fans of the late, great Keith Floyd.

A day of "Good Taste" and new friends.

The previous evening out for a stroll towards the vines above our apartment at the end of the Rue Des Charmots we met the manager/caretakers of the property we are renting. We chatted about the winemakers in the village and they told us of a family they know well of Domaine Michel Rebourgeon. Michel is retired and the father of Delphine who is married to Steve, an Englishman from Lancashire so a northerner like myself and they run the whole operation themselves with one of their sons, William. We decided to pay them a visit that morning followed by a second visit to the Nuiton Beaunoy cooperative in Beaune to taste their white wines this time. It was also time to make some decisions about what to buy to take home whether that be for everyday drinking, special occasions, or laying down to mature ..... 3,4,5 stars respectively. We planned the day with a breakfast at the Hotel-Bar-Restaurant du Pont in the village on the main road opposite the Michel Rebourgeon property, then to drive to Volnay to pick up the case of Aligote I'd bought yesterday. So an hour and a half later we had eaten the standard croissant and baguette plus coffee for breakfast, collected our wine from Volnay and dropped it off at the apartment. We now spent 30mins or so wandering around the village finding a heck of a lot of vignerons including another Rebourgeon vigneron, and a wine boutique that sold only wines from Pommard winemakers, which I suppose is a kind of cooperative outlet for wines made by the vignerons themselves rather than pooling their grapes at a traditional cooperative.

At 11am we arrived at the entrance to Domaine Michel Rebourgeon, stepped through the large open double doors which triggered a bell ringing and down some stairs came a very tall, fresh faced young man who said, "Bonjour, degustation?" and opened a door to our left. Very quickly we are conversing in English with whom we later discovered was William, older son of Delphine and Steve yet still only 18 years old. We also learned that he was studying viticulture at a wine institute in Beaune as well as working in the vineyards every spare hour!

William introduced himself, gave us a tasting/price list and asked us where we would like to start. In general their list was quite small and contained 5 Pommards, 1 Volnay, 1 Beaune, and 2 Bourgogne. I said I'd taste them all and that we should start at "the bottom" with the one white wine which was a Bourgogne Chardonnay. It was a nice everyday drinking white Burgundy, well balanced with fruit and a little acidity, some butteriness possibly from some malolactic fermentation and an absolute bargain at only €12 per bottle. You will not find a basic white

Burgundy at this price in England. (Note to self, add 12 bottles to the buy now list). Next we tasted the Bourgogne Pinot Noir, once again a classic basic Burgundy, light and fruity for everyday easy drinking and …….. Only €11 per bottle, next note to self …… buy some! This was turning out to be really interesting and a very pleasant surprise, here we had a small winemaker in the heart of Pommard fronted by a young, knowledgeable, friendly young man who is very sociable, speaks perfect English and is using a lexicon to describe his wines without a trace of "fruit salad bingo" referring only to acidity, fruitiness, tannin, balance, complexity and finish. It was at this point a lady entered who introduced herself as Delphine, Williams mother and daughter of Michel Rebourgeon. She sat down opposite us on a bench on the opposite side of the long tasting table. It was a very rustic room with old wooden furniture and whitewashed walls with large framed detailed maps of the vineyards of Beaune, Pommard and Volnay. Eventually we tasted 5 premier cru wines with two really standing out, one was a Premier Cru Volnay and the other a Pommard Premier Cru Les Rugiens, a climat we had walked alongside a couple of days ago on our trip to Volnay. William pointed out on the maps where each of their "parcels" of vines were located for the Volnay and Pommard we had just tasted, confirming the ancient inheritance or sale division of a climat into parcels or rows of vines. These two wines were absolutely stunning and matched anything we had tasted in the Nuiton Beaunoy cooperative 3 days earlier. The Volnay was €32 per bottle and the Pommard Les Rugiens was €38 per bottle, high prices you might say, but at least HALF the price you would pay in England. We discussed these two wines a lot,

I was especially interested in what the winemaker would say about the ageing potential of these wines so I could estimate their longevity and time taken to reach their peak or apogee in French winemaker speak. William and Delphine agreed that the Pommard would mature slower and last longer than the Volnay which influenced my buying decision of these 2014 vintage wines.

It was at this point that Delphine told us that their friends in Pommard, the rented property caretaker, had told them of our visit so she was interested to meet us and was genuinely complimentary of our wine knowledge. I know this wasn't mere flattery as she and William were keen to know of our interest in wine and our many travels around France. After about 10 mins of chatting she asked if we would like to see where they made the wine and explore it, and to taste from the barrels in their cellars! What an opportunity, this would be quite different from a paid visit to a chateau with a guide in a group. She told us that Steve was working in the vines at present but they could ALL meet us at 5pm at the winery if that was OK. As if we'd say "no"! It was only now I told them what wines I wanted to buy and asked if they could keep them for me for a coupe of days before our departure. This was no problem, and I ordered 12 Bourgogne Pinot Noir, 12 Bourgogne Chardonnay, 6 Pommard Premier Cru Les Rugiens, and 3 Volnay Premier Cru, all based on my earlier tasting at Nuiton Beaunoy where I now had a clear idea of the red wines I wanted from them. This was next on our days plan, off to the Beaune cooperative after a quick lunch, we had a cellar tasting to fit in!

It was an hour later we arrived at the Nuiton Beaunoy cooperative and were greeted as usual by Valerie who knew this was my white wines tasting day. Based on their wine list she had given me a few days ago I especially wanted to taste a Meursault and a St Aubin premier cru. Meursault has always been on my "potential" lists but for many years I thought it grossly overpriced, even in France. The St Aubin however was something I'd thought about after browsing the detailed maps in the World Atlas of Wine created and edited by Hugh Johnson and Jancis Robinson. If you look at the map showing Chassagne-Montrachet and Puligny-Montrachet you will find the tiny village of St Aubin and her climats/vineyards sandwiched between the two. More specifically the premier cru climat of En Remilly borders on some of the greatest white wines in Burgundy and this is often the way to find a real winner. I told Valerie what I was thinking so we dived straight in to the Meursault, a cracking wine clearly having had malolactic fermentation with a creamy buttery taste so typical. Next the St Aubin Premier Cru En Remilly 2012; my eyes must have given the game away as Valerie laughed and asked if I'd like a top up! It was all easy decision making after that and I bought 6 of the St Aubin PLUS 6 of the Pernand Vergelesses Pinot Noir tasted a few days earlier which is also a lesser known Burgundy village hidden amongst the expensive giants. Boxes loaded into the boot and we drove off for an afternoon nap before our cellar tasting at Domaine Michel Rebourgeon.

We arrived at the Rebourgeon winery at the agreed time and were met at the large entrance by William who introduced his dad, Steve Whitehead. It seemed strange to start discussing the production here with an Englishman with a Northern accent, but Steve is a very affable bloke like most of us Northerners and certainly knows his stuff having worked in the wine trade in England for many years before settling in France. He showed us briefly around the winemaking area with its large stainless steel fermentation tanks and conveyer belt for obviously feeding the grapes into the tops. I have seen some very large winemaking operations over the years and I mean no disrespect whatsoever when I say that this is quite small and definitely a family run concern, as Steve explained how he and William do literally everything in all seasons, all weathers, pruning, tying, trimming, spraying, burning, fermenting, testing, storing, bottling labelling etc etc etc. Finally we descended down some stairs and into a relatively small cellar containing perhaps 30 oak barrels, all labelled with chalk writing showing the climat and the vintage.

The previous years vintage was there for Volnay, Pommard and Bourgogne wines which Steve said we should taste and judge whether it was ready for bottling. As if I would know! So, armed with his large glass dipstick pipette William took out the bung of the first barrel, dipped it and with his thumb over the top drew out a quantity of wine. He now released some into each of our glasses, bright red, clear, but frothy. It is one of the best sights I have ever seen, a Pommard Premier Cru that 12 months ago had been Pinot Noir grapes hanging on bunches in a field in France, then crushed and fermented before being placed into this barrel. So many decisions and actions in between. It was tannic and acidic, not unpleasantly so because there was lots of red fruit flavours backing up, I can taste it now 4 years later as I write this, an experience everyone who loves wine should try. To be honest I have no idea how they were judging whether to bottle or not, I was included in all of the conversations as we sampled each barrel but I was happy to give my views on the main taste factors and shut up after that. I think we tasted from 8 different barrels as my poor teetotal wife sat on the steps and watched the boys having fun with their toys.

Each year we go back Steve or William invite me for another barrel tasting, on one occasion with my daughter and her husband who rate it as one of the best wine experiences they've ever had. I still can't work out how they decide about bottling, but I CAN decide what a good wine tastes like and what a good hard working vigneron family look like.

Bar 66, Epoisses, and a hospital visit!

The previous evening we reflected on the two sessions we'd had with the Rebourgeon family, an experience we wanted to savour over the next couple of days and believing that if we visited another vigneron so soon we'd be disappointed. So, we decided to have two fairly "quiet days" firstly in the centre of Beaune and secondly in the nearby village of Meursault.

Early morning we drove into Beaune and parked in our usual place half way around the ring road, walking up towards Place Carnot where we would spend most of the day. First up was a "hospital visit", don't panic, it was an exploration of the Hotel-Dieu Hospice de Beaune. This hospital was founded in 1443 to give relief to the poor and has been wonderfully preserved architecturally with its Burgundian tiled roofs and internally with kitchens, apothecary and wards. It also owns, as a foundation, 60 hectares of vines making extremely prestigious wines which are auctioned every November for charity. We spent about 90mins here in absolute wonder at the splendour of the place, it's history and its connection to wine, which is why I'm not going to write any more here! Later in this book you will find a chapter on the connections between wine, history, and the history of wine, so if you want immediate details skip ahead now! Or, you can read a little more on the Beaune Tourism website link I have provided in the References & Links section.

Lunch time in France means just that! Everything stops for lunch, which included two of the central shops we wanted to visit, and the cafes and restaurants fill up. So at 11.45 we strolled around Place Carnot trying to decide which one to walk into. It was still quite hot so we didn't want a 3 course Prix Fixe menu but we knew some places with good a la carte choices. One is on a corner of Place Carnot, the Grand Cafe de Lyon and we walked towards it from the opposite corner along the line of half a dozen brasseries with outdoor tables set for lunch and smartly dressed waiters standing by invitingly. Most were deserted but would be full by 12.15, though this meant we could easily see inside each one as we walked past and this led to our making a great discovery. It was *Bar 66,* a brasserie rather than a restaurant and as far as we could tell selling fromage and charcuterie boards rather than hot food, all cut, carved and chopped freshly before your eyes. We immediately decided this was the place for lunch to include some good wine too, because looking at the chalkboards on the wall everything was local, as you'd expect, but the range was brilliant from simple Bourgogne rouge ou blanc, through to the likes of Gevrey-Chambertin and Puligny-Montrachet and all served by the glass if you wished. Try and find that in England!

As soon as we walked in and sat down on a lovely sofa a young waitress came across, said Bonjour, and soon recognised us as being English. She placed down a large wine glass loaded with cheesy pastry sticks and a couple of menus showing the charcuterie boards and wine. I ordered a large glass of Meursault, Champa ordered a Badoit Rouge, and we decided on a large charcuterie platter for two. As we waited for our drinks to arrive, the only other person in the brasserie sitting at the end of the bar with a cup of coffee looked across to us, nodded and said Bonjour Madame, Monsieur, smiled, and raised his cup of coffee as if toasting us! We later discovered he was the owner of the place, and once again consider if this is the welcome one gets in bars in England these days. It seemed as if people here were pre conditioned to be extra civil to a couple of old fogies such as us! Anyway, I followed up with a glass of Beaune Premier Cru to accompany the charcuterie which was absolutely brilliant, and we sat there for quite some time as the place filled up completely with every seat taken both inside and outside in the Place Carnot. Needless to say we have since been back many times.

With lunch concluded we started on the main business of the afternoon, shopping around the wonderful wine related shops of the town centre plus a very special cheese shop. First it was into Athenaeum, a very large and difficult shop to describe, but if you're looking for any book related to Burgundy and wine, or any wine related gadget, THIS is the place. The gadgets and glassware range is astounding; decanters of all shapes and sizes, wine glasses for all grape types and occasions, aerators, pourers, stoppers, coolers, corkscrews and some openers that don't look like corkscrews at all, maps, posters and coasters, it just goes on and on. Then there are wine cards, wine games and wine quizzes. There is one room which is also a wine shop selling some very classy Burgundies, and another area selling speciality teas which keeps my wife occupied choosing the best Japanese teas she can find, especially the green teas of Matcha and Sencha. It is so tempting to spend a fortune in here, especially to a wino like me, but I try hard to have one thing in mind before I walk in then to seek out the best option, buy it, then browse a little more vowing not to return to the checkout. It works. Sometimes!

Finally, the cheese shop, Alain Hess, probably the best cheese shop in the world! We were seeking out some Epoisses de Bourgogne, a rather smelly soft cheese made from cows milk and washed with Marc de Bourgogne to form an orange coloured soft rind. It is made in the village of Epoisses situated to the north of Burgundy between Dijon and Auxerre, which at one time was also the location of the Abbeye de Citeaux whose monks supposedly originated the making of this cheese. Citeaux Abbey is no longer in Epoisses however, having relocated to near Nuits St George's in the 18th Century when for a while the manufacture died out. However it was reborn after WW2 and is now justifiably famous and to some, is known as "the king of all cheeses". The Alain Hess cheese shop is situated in the middle of the Place Carnot and well worth popping in even if all you do is look and sniff. The range of cheeses is truly phenomenal, all colours, shapes and sizes made from the milk of cows, goats and sheep. Do try it, take your time, ask questions but do a little research first and you will be well rewarded. Needless to say, they have a wine section too and will happily help you matching cheese to wine. In the case of an Epoisses, the best choice is a Sauternes from the Bordeaux region, an extremely sweet dessert white wine. So, what did we buy? Three "rounds" well wrapped to survive the journey home in a cooler box so as not to bring Eurotunnel to a halt.

Reflections in Meursault

Meursault was the first wine village in which we ever spent a night and it seemed fitting that our last day of this holiday should be spent here, reflecting on the next few days and planning our next trip.

I phoned William at Domaine Rebourgeon to let him know we would pick up our wine purchases at 5pm, and after a breakfast at the apartment we drove into the centre of Meursault just a couple of miles away. There was easy parking in the market place and we began our stroll around this famous wine village. We had just a couple of places to look at with no wine tastings in mind. First, we walked past the church downhill and round a couple of bends to the Chateau de Meursault, a really famous centre and winemaker in the area. It was an impressive looking place though fairly quiet, but it was only 10.30am! I then did something rather childish I suppose, I ran back up to the village where I'd parked the car and drove it back down in front of the chateau for a photo.

Quite a nice momento with the Jag and no other cars or people in sight. We reparked the car and then walked behind the Mairie (town hall) and down to the vineyards which sloped up and away from us towards the top of a hill, left and right for many a mile, a glorious sight in the mid morning sunshine.

Turning round we walked back up to the village alongside some large houses and stopped by some large gates, this was another group rented by Burgundy Properties, the same folks managing the Pommard apartment of this week. We had seen these on their website and wanted to see the exact location and aspect to help our decision making. It was looking good, something to reflect on.

We decided to spend some time sitting in the sun at La Place in the market place just along from the Casino Supermarket. It looks like a newsagent, which it is, as well as being a tabac, a cafe, and a wine bar. So, we got some seats outside and enjoyed a glass of Meursault and a Badoit Rouge in the warm sunshine and arrived at these thoughts on the week:

1. It really wasn't about the wine! So many things to see and do in a wine region like this; food, history, culture ….

2. We made some great new discoveries; Bar 66 a lovely place to sit and cogitate, Domaine Michel Rebourgeon as such a welcoming family, an exciting new vigneron to see and explore at Domaine Francois Gaunoux.

3. We will return next year, (2017), possibly for two weeks, probably staying in Meursault.

4. We want to explore the southern part of the Cote de Beaune especially Puligny Montrachet and Santenay.

5. All winemakers are definitely not equal.

And so after a lunch at Auberge des Vignes on the outskirts of Volnay and collecting our wines from William in Pommard …….. A good sleep and home we went. We WILL return!

Chapter 9
2017, Burgundy, Meursault

A Grande arrival!

Meursault is one of those iconic places that will always be associated with wine, and Chardonnay in particular. It's the same with Chablis, another small village 80 miles north of Meursault, with both names occupying the largest amount of space on the label of ANY of their wines before you find the name of the climat, and you will have to look on the label at the back to even find the grape variety. But there again you're supposed to know it can only be chardonnay, the queen of grapes. This years main wine holiday was based in Meursault, a decision we took during the final day of our holiday in Pommard last year, and it was going to be very special for several reasons.

We had booked two weeks through Holiday Lettings again and had chosen a two bedroom house, Chez Hall-La Grange, which was a large converted barn adjoining Chez Hall in the centre of the village. With a couple of weeks to go before arrival it appeared that disaster had struck when we had an email from the property manager telling us there had been a fire and the buildings roof had been destroyed! It was only in the second half of the email did I find that we were being offered Chez Hall-La Grande

Maison, a 17th century winemakers home with three en suite bedrooms and much more and at no extra cost to us:

"The style of La Grande Maison is French elegance at its best. From the impressive panelled reception hall with its crystal chandelier, the graciously curved stone staircase, to the quality furnishings and antique furniture the overriding sense is one of a high standard of workmanship."

We would not be on our own this year; two close friends from Cumbria, Janice and Don would be joining us for the second week, and for the first week our daughter Sharon and her husband Michael would be arriving too. They were already 3 days ahead of us in France, both keen cyclists who were riding L'Etape du Tour, a special event where amateur riders get the chance to ride a fully organised stage of the world famous Tour de France just two days before the pros would ride the same stage. This year it was a 180km high mountain passes stage in the French Alps and I confess to wondering if they would spend the whole week sleeping, but I needn't have been concerned as they spent the week wining, dining and ...... cycling around the vineyards!

Naturally there was lots of family and friends stuff going on over these two weeks and I'll try not to bore you with any of this. Also naturally we spent some time revisiting favourite haunts and friends in the area already described in a previous chapter such as Nuiton Beaunoy the fantastic wine cooperative with our friend Valerie, the Cellier Volnaysien wine boutique and restaurant owned by dear Natalie, and of course our favourite vignerons the Rebourgeon family in Pommard. But I will only describe visits here briefly as they occurred.

Sharon and Michael arrived at La Grande Maison about an hour after ourselves to find us still "in shock" at the magnificence of the property which was on 3 floors and had a massive stone balcony overlooking vineyards, but also had a gas fired barbecue and a pizza oven built into one wall as well as very comfortable outdoor furniture. The interior .... best described by the words on Holiday Lettings:

"The open plan, spacious, fully equipped gourmet kitchen features a Lacanche oven and a zinc-topped work table with inset stone pastry board. There is a special double width fridge, two dishwashers, coffee machines, ice cream maker, blender, mixers and a toaster. Continuing the open plan of this floor there is a magnificent dining table seating up to 12 then a lounge designed for comfort, with an open fireplace, and including TV receiving UK and French channels, DVD player, i-pod docking station."

We sat together on the balcony for an hour, opened a bottle of Meursault left by the owners for us, and drank it just staring at the miles of vineyards extending to our right towards Pommard and to our left towards Puligny

Montrachet, Chassagne Montrachet and Santenay. We began our planning!

In the beginning there was a convent

The first full day of many of our self catering holidays are spent food shopping, and around here that means visiting Beaune .... again. But today, although we were going into Beaune for supplies, we intended to visit one of the largest and oldest wine negociants in Burgundy, Patriarche Pere & Fils for a tour of their cellars.

Walking between the open wrought iron gates of Patriarche takes you into a courtyard that just reeks of history, and a few minutes online research had prepared us for the fact that these magnificent buildings were once a convent. It's worth mentioning again that many of our visits, or a significant part of them, invoke our mantra "it's not about the wine", and despite the fact that a tasting of wine WOULD be involved here it was not what we were mostly mindful of as we walked into Patriarche's large shop and reception area. We already knew that this place had been a convent since 1632 and that the nuns had possessed about 10 hectares of vineyards, so clearly could make use of the tunnels beneath the convent. Some of these tunnels date back to the 13th century and today stretch out for 5km across and around Beaune. Hopefully we wouldn't have to walk the full distance to get out again!

Patriarche the winemaker comes onto the scene in 1780 when a young 22 years old Jean Baptiste Patriarche founded his own winemaking company, but it wasn't until 1792 that he bought the convent and turned it into a cloth factory, but this failed, so Jean used part of the buildings for his own home and wine business. All of this was handed down through different generations of Patriarche, until the business was sold to Andre Boisseaux in 1941 who made it one of the most important wine houses in Burgundy. Finally the whole business was acquired by the French wine group Castel in 2011 for an estimated 90 million Euros!

Having each paid our €13 fee for the self guided tour it begins by walking the length of The Great Cask Room (self explanatory) before arriving in the Baroque chapel built in the mid 1800s with well preserved frescoes and wall paintings. Already one can feel "the marriage between wine and culture" as the tour leaflet mentions. A left turn and down some steps and we are into the cellars. Now, I could take a simplistic view here and say that we walked down lots of dark tunnels with lots of bottles and barrels, drank some wine and then continued back up and out into the sunlight, but I won't! Knowing the age of the building, the even older age of the tunnels and the history since 22 years old Jean Baptiste Patriarche created the wine business here in 1780, you'd have to be an ice-block not to at least mindfully consider these things as you progress, especially stopping at the 4 well placed video presentations on a loop. There are carvings in the stone, small sculptures in alcoves and thousands and thousands of bottles which must be worth as much as the Castel Group paid for the whole business! Most of the tunnels are relatively narrow, just enough room for two people to pass, but all well lit in a yellow-amber light. Eventually one arrives at a wider space with an end-on barrel with a couple of opened bottles just waiting for us, two whites, a Monthelie and a Chassagne Montrachet. Time to put those small tastevin we were given to good use, lovely! We walked on and came to another chamber with bottles on a barrel, a Pommard, a Nuits St Georges and a Gevrey Chambertin, all stunning wines to try, they clearly weren't skimping on what they gave us. Remember we were serving ourselves so could take refills as much as you wanted, a sommelier was wandering between the chambers to give any advice or information but NOT to police portion control. We all enjoyed our subterranean meandering immensely, I would really recommend doing this as the self-guided option because then you can move at your own pace .... but the key to real enjoyment is to do a little research first.

Vines, lines and wines

A couple of days later we drove to Pommard just a couple of miles away, parked in the town centre and began to walk towards Volnay through the vines. We were on a mission to try and find the exact line where geologically and geographically Pommard becomes Volnay, and also to return to the brasserie and tasting room of Domaine Francois Gaunoux we discovered last year and gave the name "Fred's Place".

The line between the two villages, Pommard and Volnay is really important. In a later chapter I will write about the effect of terroir on viticulture in more detail, but soil is an important aspect of terroir, and at this line the soil changes from iron rich clay to well drained limestone. From the World Wine Atlas we could see that the line runs uphill and across the Les Chanlins climat/field, so we looked for stone markers, walls, signs, and even started to look at the soil surface. We reached a point where we couldn't stop laughing at ourselves, 4 wine nerds grubbing around in the soil between millions of vines! It was lunchtime, so we walked on towards Volnay then down to Pavillon de Francois Gaunoux, better known to us as Fred's Place. It's nice to be instantly recognised when you've only met someone once and a year ago, but maybe that's part of the art of a waiter running a brasserie. Fred welcomed us, introduced himself to our daughter and her husband, and placed us at a table inside and away from the hot sun. We told Fred we'd like a tasting of some of Gaunoux's Meursault and he brought three bottles, all well chilled:

- Meursault, Clos de Tavaux, 2013
- Meursault 1er Cru, La Goutte d'Or, 2013
- Meursault, Clos des Meix Chavaux, 2013

The 2 clos (walled) climat wines were monopoles meaning that Gaunoux own the whole area within the walled enclosure and this always increases the value of the wine. They were all great examples of complex honeyed chardonnay from Meursault of such high quality we all found it hard to distinguish them, but the two that seemed to be best value were the two monopoles and so I bought 3 of each at €35 per bottle. As we were eating lunch, into the brasserie came the current owner of the domaine, Claudine Gaunoux, with her husband and two teenage children. They were unloading boxes of wine from a truck and as they finished Fred introduced us as friends of the Domaine Rebourgeon family in Pommard. Of course they all know each other, often caring for rows of vines next to each other, and before we knew it Claudine had asked Fred to pour us each a glass of her Pommard 1er Cru Grand Epenots 2014, a really classy Burgundian Pinot Noir. Of course I bought 3 at €45 per bottle. I chatted with Claudine for a while, telling her that our first visit to Meursault had been in 1987 over the weekend of the Meursault wine festival. I showed her copies of two photos I had taken of our family together under a festival banner showing the date and she became really excited, asking me for copies to show her father which was a simple thing to do between iPhones. I've since learned how committed Claudine is to Meursault, Burgundy, and her vines, and how she has resisted selling any of her vineyards for a large fortune. She believes that she is the guardian of the domaine on behalf of all of the Gaunoux generations before her as well as her children coming after her. Her passion is tangible and in a way that some would find aggressive, but not us, this is our kind of winemaker!

Puligny-Montrachet

Sharon and Michael took off for an early morning bike ride to Puligny-Montrachet on their penultimate day before heading off to their home in Cheltenham. It was another lovely sunny morning and Champa and I sat out on the balcony eating breakfast after a short walk to the boulangerie. It was a clear blue sky, perfect for sitting outside rather than walking through underground cellars or long drives and we were wondering how best to fill the day. The best ideas are often the simplest, and when Sharon returned she told us of how nice the area around Puligny was and how that it had a nice central Place/ square with a restaurant and wine bar. So, after a lazy morning we drove to Puligny-Montrachet, had a bit of a walk around, then found a table for lunch at L'Estaminet des Miex.

A little iPhone research told us how the two rival winemaking villages of Puligny and Chassagne are separated by a small hill, Mont Rachaz , literally meaning "the scabby hill" and on which each village had vines planted. Eventually the two villages appended the name of THEIR hill to the village name, hence Puligny-Montrachet and Chassagne-Montrachet! The rivalry goes further as wines from the Chassagne side of the hill are labelled Le Montrachet whereas wines from the Puligny side are labelled simply as Montrachet with "no need" for "Le"!

The first part of our plan was to have a traditional lunch followed by some time at the rather posh looking wine bar at the head of the Place on the opposite side of the roundabout. The four of us shared two Boeuf Bourgignon and two Jambon Persille, three portions of chips and one of rice. No wine, just a carafe of water and a couple of cokes. All very relaxing in a well laid out restaurant with half of it being "outdoors" with glass or perspex sides for wind protection, and the interior being classical rural French with solid tables covered with colourful tablecloths. The food, service and general ambience were all excellent and we made a note to return here with our Cumbrian friends the following week. We walked around the Place de Marronniers, (chestnut trees) past the hotel and restaurant Le Montrachet, along a row of magnificent stone built houses, and up to the roundabout at the head of the Place where the D113A meets the D113B, and had a really good look at the superb sculpture arrangement in the centre of the roundabout.

It comprises 4 people, men and women, in what looks like traditional agriculture dress and forged or sculpted in bronze. It was a few strides from here into the Cave de Puligny Montrachet, a shop, wine bar, and brasserie all in one with a great wine list and cold food platters of charcuterie and/or cheeses. We seated ourselves around a low table on comfortable armchairs in the outer area looking out towards the sculpture and the lines of chestnut trees around the Place. We ordered a bottle of Puligny Montrachet 2013 from Domaine J Pascal at €35 and it arrived well chilled in a heart shaped bowl of ice. Now if that seems expensive to you, then be aware that it sells from a number of UK wine merchants at around £35 per bottle, so that's quite a good price sitting in a wine bar in Burgundy! In fact we constantly find this, that the price of a wine in French restaurants and brasseries local to the growing region is always reasonably priced, and in a subsequent chapter we have a similar tale of a very special bottle of Chablis in a restaurant in the village of Chablis itself.

This was a real treat, sitting in the village of Puligny Montrachet, drinking a bottle of Puligny Montrachet, together as a family. Could chardonnay ever get better than this? Probably not, because that bottle of chardonnay has since become our benchmark for the style of chardonnay we like, lightly oaked, perfectly balanced and with a long finish. Pure ELEGANCE!

A symbol of Burgundy
The second week of our Meursault holiday began by entertaining our Cumbrian friends with "the usual" trips and tours around Beaune, the cooperative Nuiton Beaunoy, Pavillon Francois Gaunoux, and Domaine Michel Rebourgeon. But one of the visits we'd saved for this week was to the Chateau de La Rochepot, an easy drive from Meursault to St Aubin and then just a few miles beyond. It's described as being "a symbol of burgundy" and I guess that must have a lot to do with its general architecture and that the original dates back to the year 1180, but there's some more recent history that they might prefer to keep quiet, though I didn't find out about it until 3 years after our visit! Be patient!

The chateau towers over the tiny village of Rochepot in a strategic defensive position high up on a rocky hillside, not typical of many French chateau that were more palaces on river banks or the edge of lakes and not designed as fortresses. Another difference we discovered once inside, is that this chateau DOES have furnishings and artefacts which is so unlike the majority of French chateau which are either completely bare, or have displays of paintings, pottery, or other art and craftwork that seem to have no connection with the place whatsoever.

Back to the history however which explains some of the internal furnishing. The first chateau was owned by Seigneur de Montagu Alexander who was the son of the Duke of Burgundy, but a couple of centuries or so later in 1403 it was bought by Regnier Pot, a returning crusader knight and Chamberlain to the Duke of Burgundy. Regnier Pot then renamed it from being Chateau de La Roche Nolay to .... Chateau de La Roche Pot! Nothing like naming a chateau after yourself in those days to demonstrate power and prestige I suppose. Also at that time Pinot Noir grapes were planted nearby which was a decree from Philip the Bold, Duke of Burgundy a few years earlier. Ownership of the chateau passed from one aristocrat to another across the next 300 years and included Anne de Montmorency the Marshal of France, followed by the Cardinal de Retz, then the President of the Burgundy Parliament. Remember that France was not a single nation in those days and Burgundy was one of the most powerful states in Europe. During the French Revolution around 1790 the chateau was seized as a national asset, partially destroyed by vandals and fell into disrepair until being bought in 1893 by Cécile Carnot who was the wife of the French President. It was her son, Sadi, who carried out a 26 year long restoration of the chateau highlighting much of its splendour reminiscent of the times of Regnier Pot, which in my opinion is a fitting tribute to the man himself and also the first planting of Pinot Noir in the area.

We had left Meursault mid morning with Janice and Don who had arrived a few days earlier in their two seater Audi Quattro, meaning that by now I was close to buying a bus conductors cap and a ticket machine for entry to my much larger Jaguar XF! A sunny day and a route taking us via the wine villages of Puligny Montrachet and St Aubin meant lots of stops for photos and constant marvelling at the diligence of lone vignerons toiling in row after row of vines. Apparently it takes two vines worth of grapes to create one bottle of wine here which undoubtedly partly accounts for the intensity of their superb chardonnay wines. Approaching Rochepot the views of the Chateau are really spectacular and after a few minutes we have parked at the top of the hill alongside the Chateau entrance. The entry fee was a reasonable €8 and a free guide booklet was provided in English which, as usual, I didn't look at until we got back to Meursault! Why DO I keep doing that? Anyway we entered via a drawbridge and through an arch with the Rochepot coat of arms above us, and what really strikes you initially is the typical Burgundian roofs of coloured tiles and the pointed conical grey turrets.

I'm sure that if you saw a photo of a building with the classical yellow/amber tiles you would know immediately that it is somewhere in Burgundy. At ground level the rooms were restored during the 19th century so the artefacts in the kitchen and great hall are from that period rather than being medieval, but that's ok because the effect is certainly one of opulence, power and wealth. The main areas of interest though are architectural as you ascend to other floors via narrow spiral stone stairways and follow the walls via wooden platforms and walkways. In the upper levels you can appreciate that this really was built as a fortress as well as being a place to be lived in comfortably. One surprise was a room in an upper level tower is .... The Chinese Room, furnished with ornaments and a large Buddha as gifts to President Sadi Carnot from the last Empress of China, Tseu-Hi.

So now, the "latest piece of history" from Chateau de La Rochepot I only discovered on writing this chapter three years later. In 2014 the Chateau was put up for sale at just over €3.2 million and was bought by a Ukrainian, Dmitry Malinovski, so he was the owner in 2017 when we visited. But ...... in 2018 Malinovski was arrested after an investigation into corruption and money laundering schemes in which he purchased and lived in the castle after faking his own death!

Anyway, completely oblivious to all of this, we left after an hour or so of exploration and settled down in Puligny Montrachet for the afternoon with a lunch at Estaminet (again!) and a tasting flight of six white wines at the usual Caveau de Puligny Montrachet which rounded off the day nicely. I could live here, mind you I say that about everywhere in Burgundy!

No need to spit!

On the last day of our friends week with us Don offered to drive me to Santenay, a village south of Meursault where he had noticed a winemaker tasting room in the town square from a drive through with Janice earlier that morning. A good chance at last to get a ride in their two seater and not be lumbered with driving back after tasting a dozen wines. No need to spit!

Geographically as an introduction to wine tasting in Burgundy, it doesn't come much better than Santenay, a lovely place to start your wine travels moving south to north through better known ….. but more expensive wine areas. Here's a quote from The World Atlas of Wine:

"After the hamlet of Haut-Santenay and the little town of Bas-Santenay, the Cote half turns to take up its characteristic slope to the east. This southern end of the Cote de Beaune is the most confused geologically and in many ways is atypical of the Cote as a whole. Complex faults in the structure of the hills make radical changes of soil and subsoil in Santenay. Part of the commune is analogous to parts of the Cote de Nuits giving deep flavoured …. red wine. Other parts give light wine more typical of the Cote de Beaune."

We were welcomed at Domaine Mestre, which is in the town square of Santenay, by a delightful lady now retired, but who works in the tasting room on Sundays to give the Mestre family a day off. She had worked for them full time for many years, but it wasn't until we had left I realised I didn't know her name! Not very mindful on my part at all!

We tasted our way through 8-10 wines, white and red, village and Premier Cru as we listened to the explanations about three Climats in particular, the three Premier Cru Climats of Beaurepaire, Passe-Temps, and Clos Faubard. They are all shown in The World Atlas of Wine, and although not highlighted by Jancis Robinson as "the best" in Santenay, they all represented good value for money at around £20 per bottle 2013, 2014 and 2011 vintages respectively.

Poor old Don really had to hold back as he was driving, so most of the photos he took with my camera whilst only tasting a couple himself. He really must learn to spit more! Anyway, at the end of a very pleasant Sunday afternoon my personal collection grew by a dozen each of Santenay Beaurepaire 2013 (white), Santenay Passe-Temps 2014 (white), and Santenay Clos Faubard 2011 (red). Clearly the whites were chardonnay and the reds pinot noir. All good examples of Domaine Mestre and their Santenay wines ...... highly recommended with my rating at the end of the wine tasting being 4 stars for each of the three wines I bought. And why do I recommend that you begin your wine travels through Burgundy here? Simply because you can experience white and red, chardonnay and pinot noir, light and heavier, varying style and terroir ALL in the same village, all grown around the village. Here it seems less formal and less intimidating than the better known villages and towns of the Côte-d'Or, I know it's all in the mind but it's important that folks who are new to visiting regions and vigneron feel comfortable from the start.

On reflection

This had been a very relaxing and interesting wine related holiday for a number of different reasons, some related to family and close friendships, the renewal of "wine friendships" in Burgundy, and one or two new discoveries. But a couple of other things had piqued my interest caused by questions put to me during the past two weeks. The first and almost the simplest to answer at the time was "how big is your collection and how do you decide what to buy and when to drink"? The more I thought about it the more I realised that my collection building strategy was quite haphazard and worth a review. The second question was "how many different grapes have you tasted?", and I had to answer that I had absolutely no idea .... but it pushed me to find out. The third question was "how many different countries have you visited and/or tasted their wines?". This last question set my thinking back to 40+ years ago when as students a group of us formed a small wine club and began tasting wines from different countries, but mostly we focused on international grapes, such as Chardonnay, Cabernet Sauvignon, Pinot Noir etc etc rather than exploring grape varieties indigenous to a particular country. Now, if you think about it these three questions are connected and this realisation was bugging me all the way home! It affected our next two years of wine travels, AND the collecting and drinking of wine at home, and I'll describe this as an introduction to further wine travels of 2018 and 2019.

Chapter 10
Grapes, Bottles and Wines

Grapes 100: "How many different grapes have you tasted"?

In the chapter "Early Learning" I related how my earliest memory of buying a bottle of wine was of a Hirondelle Red as a student in Glasgow in the late 1960s. It cost 2s/6d or 12.5p in today's money and was made in Austria, subsequently prosecuted for indoctrinating wines with ethylene glycol! My **latest** purchase is of a case of Pommard, Les Rugiens from Domaine Rebourgeon at €46 per bottle! How times change, as well as one's palate and the size of your wallet!

Pinot Noir is my favourite grape and Burgundy my favourite region to visit and buy from. Pommard and Volnay in the Cote de Beaune are my two favourite villages. My favourite white grape is the Chardonnay, but also only from Burgundy with my favourite wine villages for it being Meursault, Puligny Montrachet, and Santenay. Come to think of it I also like St Aubin, Montagny and Chablis! Now you may be wondering why I'm beginning with such anecdotes and the short answer is in my desire to become a member of **The Wine Century Club** once I had learned of its existence in late 2017. To quote from their website:

"The Wine Century Club is for adventurous wine lovers

worldwide. If you've tasted at least 100 different grape varieties, you're qualified to become a member. If you haven't tried 100 different grape varieties, but are interested in the concept, you're welcome to all of our events. Please join us in promoting the awareness of uncommon wine grape varieties. We currently have 1,740 members worldwide."

I discovered that there were only 62 members in the UK and .... I hoped to become the 63rd. At the time I HAD tasted close to 100 varieties of grape but didn't know it, even though my *current* preference is quite narrow relating to Burgundy Pinot Noir and Chardonnay.

Moving on, as soon as I read about The Wine Century Club I began scouring through my old wine logs back to 1981 to note all of the wines, and therefore grapes, I had tasted. It came to around 40, but I knew there was more because of wines I had tasted during holidays in Alsace, Loire, Jura, and the extremely diverse region of Languedoc. Then there were recent holidays in Spain and Portugal. That easily doubled my list.

But what finally got me over the finishing line was purchasing a case of red and a case of white Italian wines from The Wine Society, deliberately chosen to explore new grapes, blends and regions. At last, 100+ grapes from the "old world" of Europe as I sent off my application to join The Club. I received my certificate and been accepted as a member of the exclusive Wine Century Club in early 2018. It had taken me 50 years to achieve this and required a very high level of education, lots of money, worldwide travel, fitness and stamina and a tender palate with a stomach of iron. I also needed a wife who could drive but who didn't drink, but this was NOT why I married Dr C 48 years ago!

I won't list the 110 grapes I've tasted, but here's an alphabet soup of grapes many tasted over the years without a mention of Chardonnay Sauvignon Blanc Shiraz Cabernet Sauvignon Merlot Old Uncle Tom Cobbley:

- A is for Aligote, the forgotten white grape of Burgundy
- B is for Baga, the red grape in Portuguese wines from Barraida
- C is for Corvina, the red grape in many Italian Valpolicella wines
- D is for Dolcetto, the red grape in Italian wines from Piedmont
- E is for No bloody idea!
- F is for Furmint, the beautiful white grape from Hungary, used in dry and sweet wines of Tokaj
- G is for the white Gruner Veltliner from Austria with the wine found in the fashionable restaurants of New York and Hong Kong
- H is for Harslevelu, another white Hungarian grape tasting like a fine Chablis
- I is for I have no idea!
- J is for Just as rare as grapes beginning with E and I!

- K is for Kekfrankos, the red Hungarian grape equivalent to the Blaufrankisch originating in Austria and also grown in Slovenia
- L is for ….. Lambrusco, yes I've drunk it too!
- M is for Marsanne the white grape from the Southern Rhône in France and used in the expensive wines of Hermitage, Crozes-Hermitage and St Joseph.
- N is for Nebbiolo, the noble grape of the red Nebbiolo wines of Italy
- O is for the white Ortega grape grown in the Mosel-Saar-Ruhr region of Germany
- P is for Pedro Ximinez, the grape of Malaga (and others) making red sweet aperitif wines
- Q is for Not a lot!
- R is for Rondinella, the red Italian grape used in Bardolino
- S is for Semillon the white grape grown mostly in Australia and France, used in dry and sweet wines, famously in Sauternes and Barsac
- T is for Tannat, the red grape of almost black tannic wines from Madiran in Languedoc/Occitanie
- U is for Usaxelauri, a red grape and I've never tasted it
- V is for verdelho, a white grape of Portugal but grown mostly on the island of Madeira
- W is for Not a clue again!
- X is for Xinomavro the red wine grape of Macedonia
- Y is Unknown to me!
- Z is for Zierfandler a red grape of Austria but used to make white wine!

So that's the first part of this chapter completed and demonstrating how much one of those questions in Meursault influenced my "wine behaviour" and it continues to this day as I seek out new grapes to try as you will read more of below and in further chapters. Now on to answering another question asked of me in Meursault.

Wines 101: "How many different countries have you visited and wines tasted"?

All three questions I was asked in Meursault got me thinking a lot about the wines I was buying and collecting, that at times was both narrow and also random. Was there anything I actually wanted to achieve, for example did I want to get to taste 200 different grapes or 300 or whatever? I quickly decided that such a proposition held no interest for me, but that maybe tasting grapes I liked already from different countries WOULD be interesting, such as Pinot Noirs from New Zealand, California, Oregon, Chile, South Africa, Australia and so on. I realised that this was leading me towards a classic Bucket List.

Bucket Lists are a bit like Marmite, love 'em or hate 'em, nothing in between! Until recently I had been in the "hate 'em" group for full blown Bucket Lists, though I freely admit to having had wish-lists for travel and mountaineering. They served their primary purpose of helping me to plan and schedule travels to USA, China, Nepal, and lots of European cities, as well as summiting quite a few peaks in the Alps and Himalaya. It also helped me to become a member of The Wine Century Club having sipped my way to having tasted 100+ different wine grapes as shown above.

So, one day browsing the shelves of our local Waterstones I spotted the book *101 Wines To Try Before You Die* by Margaret Rand and thought "hmm, that could be useful if it combines wine tasting with wine travel"! Needless to say I bought it, and a few days later my brain goes into overdrive about cost and location for #1 Domaine de Chevalier Blanc, #2 Chateau Haut-Bailly, #3 Chateau Margaux (god help me!) .... #5 Chateau d'Yquem ...... strike, already done that one, ... #7 Le Chambertin .... anyway you get the picture?

Here's what Margaret Rand says in her opening remarks to her *book:*

"These are not the most iconic wines in the world, nor the 101 highest-scoring wines in the world, though many of them are iconic and many are high scoring. They are the wines that have given me the greatest pleasure. If there is a thread running through these choices it is one of balance, elegance, poise and precision."

I like that: BALANCE, ELEGANCE, POISE, PRECISION and I will try hard to use it as a yardstick as I taste my way around them.

I decided to conduct my wine tasting of these 101 Wines as much in-situ with the wine producer as possible so that the exercise becomes linked with our wine travels, especially around Europe. Where impossible I decided to just use my Wine Searcher app to find the best value source to purchase it. Also I would not be tasting them in the strict #1 to #101 sequence either, in fact I may not even make it or try to make it to the finish line, but I decided to give it a bloody good go!

To kick off we would soon be spending some time in France again, particularly in Chablis and Alsace, so .... opportunity knocks for quite a few wines in the book.

Sadly, it didn't quite work like that, because while it may be interesting to some folks who like reading other's views on the best 101 wines to try .... it started to prove impossible to actually get some of these wines without paying a fortune in shipping costs, or to even visit a winemaker to buy some when you were standing outside his door! A case in point is the Chablis Grand Cru "Les Clos" from Vincent Dauvissat, a winemaker who it is impossible to visit, contact, or even to find a bottle of the stuff in a shop in Chablis itself! I respect Mr Dauvissat's desire for reclusiveness despite his rock star status, but the wild goose chase and potential expense of finding a bottle was too much for yours truly. He wouldn't even sell a bottle to a friend of mine who lives in Chablis!

There were other similar examples we came across, Dagueneau Pouilly-Fume Silex, the wines of Phillipe Alliet in Chinon .... but I think you've got my point, the book is quite impractical because I would die long before I could get anywhere near many of these wines, despite being able to afford them!

So I decided to adapt my Wines101 "travel", but not always visiting vineyards of interest. This almost negates my maxim of "Its not about the wine" because I buy a wine and end up drinking it alone at home. It's not quite the same as trying a Dauvissat Chablis in a Chablis bistro or visiting the Furstentum vineyard for a Gewürztraminer. Equally, the vast majority of the wines in the 101 book are just not available, so I'm trying a new tack. I now use the Wines 1001 book and buy from recommended vineyards via the Wine Society or reputable U.K. wine merchants even if I can't find the actual wine listed. It's not quite the same, but it's an interesting exercise.

But, I don't want to lose your interest here because we DID manage to find a way around the Dauvissat Chablis problem as well as visiting Furstentum in Alsace, Clos du Papillon in Loire, Clos de L'Echo in Loire all of which were part of our 2018 travels in France. In addition many more have been tasted as part of the global travel from the armchair in my Wines 101 Room in our Cotswolds home and I will describe these also in a separate chapter.

Bottles 200: "How big is your collection and how do you decide what to buy"?

Back to those three question asked of me in Meursault one of which was about about wine collecting, but although below I answer the question specifically, I hope you are starting to realise that the answers are completely intertwined, inseparable even.

Creating and maintaining ones own wine collection is one of life's greatest pleasures and .... challenges! How to begin, how many bottles, how much to spend, which wines, what types, how long to keep, how will I know a good wine to add ....? The list of questions, and therefore challenges is endless. So I'd like to share with you all here how I started and what I've built it into.

I began my collection around 40 years ago with a 12 bottle rack in the spare bedroom of our first house in North Wales. Today I have two temperature controlled wine chiller cabinets and a collection of 191 bottles categorised as Everyday (79), Premium (79), Investment (33); I will explain the categories later but it's important to know that this profile of roughly 2:2:1 has changed over the 40 years I've been collecting, and that my "wine education" began some 5 years prior to that.

Squirrels know how!

To create a collection of ANYTHING you need a level of knowledge that matches your objective and aspirations for the collection, whether it's pottery, art, furniture, silverware or wine. Naturally you have to like a wine before stocking it so prior knowledge of it is vital. Also knowing whether it will improve in taste and value is a good idea too (!) over 1, 3, 5, 10 years. You must decide whether you want it as a special occasion wine in the next couple of years, or as an investment either to sell OR to drink knowing it's now worth x2, x5, x10 etc what you paid for it originally! Conversely you don't want to buy a wine that has turned to vinegar 12 months after you bought it!

Step 1 Create A Collection Profile

This may seem an odd place to begin, at the end, but it's a bit like knowing your destination BEFORE beginning a journey. I have already mentioned my own profile above and it is based on a simple assessment system I use when tasting a wine at a restaurant, in a wine bar, or with a winemaker in his cellars, as well as tasting in my own home. Here's my simple assessment system:

⭐Undrinkable

⭐⭐Enjoyable but wouldn't buy/rebuy

⭐⭐⭐Everyday wine, rebuy

⭐⭐⭐⭐Premium wine for special occasions

⭐⭐⭐⭐⭐Investment wine for ageing/longer storage

Naturally you don't want any single star wines in your collection but you DO want to build up a proportion of Everyday, Premium and Investment wines with the initial cost of each probably increasing as you ascend the scale, but not necessarily. Don't agonise over this too much, you can split the three categories by number of bottles or by money spent. Let's say you kick off with £100, you might decide to split that money 3 ways by spending £33 on each category which might result in 5:3:2 bottles for Everyday, Premium, and Investment respectively.

So you now have 10 bottles in your collection. This is just an example, but 10 isn't many bottles and only having 2 Investment wines stored isn't going to give you a good "return", but it's not about the money! You don't have to buy 10+ bottles every time either, you might read something about a brilliant wine for £20 which will age well so go out and buy one bottle. Or, maybe it's your birthday and you ask for present(s) of a couple of Investment level wines. Of course, the trick is having the knowledge to choose the right wines to invest in!

Step 2 Choose Storage Space Wisely
Under the stairs, in your garage, in a spare bedroom, in the loft? These places MIGHT all be suitable provided some simple rules are followed, especially for wines you want to keep for some time. But certainly digging out a cellar under your dining room is not necessary. You need to understand that the Three Enemies of wine storage are .... Temperature, Light, Vibration. So, having a wine rack in the kitchen on a window ledge above your cooker is not an option! You need to find somewhere in your house that minimises the effect of all three. Under the stairs sorts out light and vibration but isn't much use if there's a radiator next to the entry. Similar with a bedroom unless you have a blackout blind on the window and switch the radiator off permanently. Short term storage of Everyday wines isn't a problem here, but Premium and Investment wines would be at risk, so choose your space wisely.

In my case for around 30 years I stored my collection in a loft space above the garage. The garage is connected to the house and I can enter this space from a door on our first floor landing. It's had extra insulation and is in total darkness. I used the common interlocking wooden racks against the walls for storing the bottles on their sides. Nowadays I have two temperature controlled wine chiller cabinets with uv light filtering glass doors, which combined can store around 200 bottles.

Step 3 Build your Knowledge, Experience, Strategy
Please don't go rushing out now and lash out £100 on 3 wines to kick off your collection! It reminds me of the joke about the old bull and his son in a field. Looking down on the cows below them, the young bull says "Quick dad, lets go down there and have sex with one of those cows each" to which the old bull replies to his son, "No son, let's take our time and have sex with them ALL"! Wine collecting is based on both cognitive and emotional features. Only buy what you like ..... you will have to drink it one day, so don't go buying some Grand Cru Burgundies with massive ageing potential if you don't like Pinot Noir. Conversely, if you really like a fruity Rose wine from the Languedoc don't buy some for Investment purposes as they're made to be drunk in 6-12 months!
Wines with ageing potential have "balance" in terms of acidity, tannin, fruit (and oak). So learning how to spot this is vital, though you could just read tasting notes from experts on a website such as Wine Searcher (https://www.wine-searcher.com) where you will also get an idea of ageing potential anyway. Supermarkets may be the best place for Everyday wines, but the better place for Premium and Investment wines will be a good reputable wine merchant (we used to use Oddbinns originally) or join the Wine Society if you're in the UK. This is also where visiting vineyards and winemakers comes into play, go and meet

them, taste their wines, ask them about ageing potential and when the wine will "peak" (apogee in French). Most are delighted to discuss this with you, go back each year and before you know it you'll have personal tastings from the barrels before bottling

There are millions of books on wine you could buy ranging from specific annual guides that give you advice on what to buy NOW, through to books on general principles and knowledge about wine. My favourite reference book is The World Wine Atlas from Jancis Robinson & Hugh Johnson, loads of stuff on grape varieties, countries, regions, winemakers, as well as maps going down to named field level!

Step 4 Monitor Your Storage and Tasting

We all make mistakes, but not learning from those mistakes is the biggest mistake of all. I've made plenty over the years when it comes to wine buying, and I still make them to this day but less often. For example I recently explored Italian wines from different regions and from different grapes, mostly with the help of Danell of Vinthropology, my sommelier friend in Italy. Some of the wines she recommended I just didn't like, too acidic for my taste and made sure this was noted in my favourite wine app, VinoCell.

But equally there were some wines new to me that I really liked, so, you win some and you lose some, but the total experience was a winner! In VinoCell you can easily enter the name and details of every wine in your collection. The more data you enter on name, vintage, winemaker, grape variety, country, district, village, peak years ... the better and easier it will be to check back through your records to see if you've had a wine before and your view of it. Also as your collection expands to a few hundred bottles finding that extra special single bottle of Burgundy for Christmas lunch gets harder unless you've logged its position in your cellar/collection.

Step 5 Which wines?
Steps 1-4 are the main factors overall in relation to creating your wine collection. I haven't mentioned budget because it's obviously a personal choice. Likewise choosing the profile and types of wine for your collection is personal choice too. In my case my whole profile is built around Burgundy, especially red wines from Pommard and white wines from Chablis. Why is this you might ask? Well firstly I like Pinot Noir and Chardonnay, especially unoaked and terroir driven wines. Secondly they are both easy and enjoyable places to visit from the UK. Finally and most importantly we have built a relationship with the owners and winemakers of Domaine Michel Rebourgeon in Pommard and Domaine des Malandes in Chablis. Also these wines age/mature really well but both domaines make wines that are early drinkers too, and cheaper, so it's possible to cover my profile from these two winemakers alone. However I also like wines made from Cabernet Franc in Chinon, from Chenin Blanc in Savennieres, from

Sauvignon Blanc in Menetou Salon and St Bris, so these all figure in my collection too. I like sparkling wines but NOT the inflated prices of champagne so I collect Cremant de Bourgogne and Cremant de Loire at a quarter of the price of Champagne when I visit Chinon and Pommard. And finally finally, my app VinoCell can also tell me how much my wine collection is worth compared to how much I paid at the time! The answer .... X4 .... not that I would ever sell anything!

So I hope this section gets you started on your collection or, dare I say it ... helps you improve an existing collection, but do please reflect on all three sections to enhance your enjoyment of wine, and this book, because they are all connected as you will see in the forthcoming chapters.

Chapter 11
2018, Burgundy, Chablis

*"Chablis's ubiquity makes it easy to forget what's amazing
about it—namely, that it's one of the greatest demonstrations of
terroir on the planet. How do we know this? Because it's one of
the few places where Chardonnay, with basic winemaking
techniques, produces a complete wine of uncommon distinction.
It's not difficult to spot the Chablis out of a flight of blind wines."*
The Sommelier's Atlas of Taste, Rajat Parr and Jordan
Mackay

Our first foray into French wine country for 2018 was
not only varied and hectic, but also enlightening and a
kickstart into my Wines 101 project. I think that "project" is
perhaps the wrong word to use because it conjures up
thoughts of a goal, a schedule and a clear organisation......
which we didn't actually have. Nevertheless we did have a
plan to visit Chablis and then Ribeauville in July 2018,
specifically to visit the vigneron and taste a Grand Cru
wine in each place. One turned out to be impossible, the
other a delightful experience that seemed as if we'd
stepped back in time a couple of centuries!

There were four of us, myself and wife Champa,
daughter Sharon and husband Michael who piled into
Sharon's BMW 4x4 at 5am and headed off towards Kent for

a journey through Eurotunnel emerging in France. Today had been planned by Sharon and it didn't involve wine or going anywhere near a wine region .... we were heading for Dunkirk. I have never been to the beaches of Dunkirk before, though my dad spent a few days here in June 1940! This is just a quick day trip, including an hour at the small Operation Dynamo Museum en route deeper into France and something I know Sharon wanted to see too in memory of her grandad, a Coldstream Guardsman in WW2, she had never met. It really was an interesting experience, though it did feel a little eerie in the museum and then standing on one of the beaches looking across the Channel to England. We had the classic Moules-Frites lunch in a beach restaurant, a somewhat quiet affair with each of us probably reflecting on those dramatic events here in 1940 and knowing that my young 23 year old dad was here, and survived. We drove on to Arras for the night which would leave us with just a 3 hour drive to Chablis the next morning.

Wines, vines, cellars and dinners

We were visiting Chablis with three days of wine tasting ahead of us with a mixture of scheduled visits to cellars, random drop-ins to a few more, and evening meals where the wine list is full of all four levels of Chablis and multiple producers! This was also the beginning of searching out my Wines 101 Bucket List, especially #1 on the list, a Chablis Grand Cru Les Clos from Domaine Dauvissat.

We arrived at around 11.30 and parked quite close to our hotel .... which was closed ..... with a sign on the door which said "Back at 2pm"! What the heck is this, I'd had trouble with the booking in the first place which I'd made direct by phone with the owner and it had taken me a couple of weeks and further phone calls to even receive confirmation. This was our third choice hotel in the village because the two best hotels were full. So, we had a 30min walk around the central area to help Sharon and Michael get their bearings before finding seats in the Chablis Bar for a glass of wine and a light lunch. This is a very friendly bar-restaurant with an outdoor seating area sheltered from the wind and a simply furnished interior. In a very short time it was full of locals for lunch, always a good sign. Just after 2pm we found the hotel open, checked in, and carried our luggage up the winding staircase to our rooms. It seemed old and tired with ancient traditional French furniture, but although the central areas seemed dusty and threadbare our rooms were OK. Breakfast was good, but we would never have stayed here unless the other hotels hadn't been full, and the next day our friend John who has a holiday home nearby told us "he felt sorry for us" having to stay here. It was Hotel Bergerand/Les Vignes de Sarah, and I believe it was up for sale at the time and I'm unsure if it even still exists as a hotel as it's not showing on Google Maps!

The Flying Winemaker

Arriving in a wine region for a holiday is usually shrouded in such anticipation that wine tastings begin before unpacking our cases in our hotel! And so it was today, have lunch, check in, drop off bags, go out the front door, turn right and onwards to Domaine des Malandes where I had an appointment with Richard Rottiers the owner. Richard can rightly be called a "flying winemaker" having zoomed off to New Zealand and South Africa a few years back to oversee development of a couple of vineyards and wineries. A recent article in an issue of Decanter magazine described him as one of the "young up and coming winemakers of ….. Beaujolais"! Eh, strange, we're going to Chablis! However, Richard actually owns vineyards in both Chablis and Beaujolais so it's possible to have a tasting of BOTH in his Chablis cellars ……. so we did!

Richard is an enthusiastic and engaging young man who clearly has vast knowledge of winemaking and infinite patience and generosity towards visitors for a wine tasting. After walking us around his production facilities we descended into his tasting room, brilliantly decorated with wall murals painted by his mother, where 9 different Chablis were ready and waiting for us.

We began however with a Sauvignon Blanc, a grape permitted to be grown in the area around the village of St Bris just outside Chablis, so simply known as Sauvignon St Bris. Now, Michael, Sharon's husband detests Sauvignon Blanc so was not best pleased …. but he tried it and was staggered! Clearly the terroir of this area plus Richard's biodynamic approach transforms the wine into something of lower acidity and no cats pee aromas! As he said, this wine should give aromas of "cassis/blackcurrant flowers" without the heavy gooseberry normally associated with it, and it sure did. One case, straight into the car. Bargain at €7.50 per bottle.

Next up was the full range of Chablis grades, starting with Petit Chablis, then Chablis, Chablis Premier Crus, and finally Chablis Grand Crus. The determining factor of each of the four grades is WHERE the vines are grown and whether the soil is Kimmeridgean, and I will write more about this below .... The Four Grades of Chablis

All of Richard's wines flex between being of high or low minerality, moderate or high complexity, medium or long finish so it becomes a question of personal taste for all of his wines made from a single grape .... the noble Chardonnay. However as you climb the grades the complexity and depth of each wine increases, as does the price, but at €13 per bottle of his "standard" Chablis 2017 this is an absolute bargain ..... another case straight into the car. Daughter now worried as she hasn't bought any yet and I'm slowly filling the boot space! Now we entered the realm of the Chablis Premier Crus and Richard opened a Vau de Vey and a Fourchaume. Absolute nectar, both of them, each different in style with the Vau de Vey having a greater minerality than the deeper flavoured Fourchaume. All a question of personal taste again, but the garbage "fruit salad" approach of many professional wine writers just doesn't interest us. These two Chablis Premier Cru are both full throttle, classy, clean-fresh, long finish highly flavoursome wines. Not even a hint of oak thank goodness, just Chardonnay in its purest form. Another case for me into the car: daughter looking more worried, I tell her to start flexing her own credit card before it's too late!

Richard now walked across to his racks and brought back one more bottle to open and taste …. my goodness, a Chablis Grand Cru, Les Clos … the wine I had as #1 on my Wines 101 Bucket List but from a different producer. If we thought the Premier Cru were nectar this was the Queen of Nectars, the initial aroma was an absolute explosion of lemony fruit, floral notes and stone …. sorry that's close to a fruit salad approach, but it's what happened. Flavour was a similar experience. But I only bought a single bottle for reasons I will also reveal below, but still a bargain at €40, and well described in The Sommelier's Atlas of Taste again:

"Les Clos The king. The biggest cru, occupying a massive swath of the hill facing just between due south and southwest, Les Clos is rocky and extremely well draining. It produces a hyper-mineral wine of enormous depth. Usually somewhat shut down and brooding for its first decade, it emerges with time to be something wonderfully complete, complex, and generous. Its wines always have notable power, length, and breadth."

Across all of these wines Richard had carefully explained precisely where the grapes had been grown, the associated terroir, how quality and flavour was affected by it, and it's comparison to previous vintages as all of these were 2017. But now it was time for a Beaujolais tasting of his Villages, Brouilly and Moulin a Vent. Quite brilliant again, so …. a case of Brouilly into the car!

Clearly we cannot recommend Richard and his Domaine des Malandes highly enough, almost certainly the best all round wine tasting we have ever experienced over 30+ years of visits to vineyards in France. Go and try it for yourself, if you visit Chablis, as the first thing you do before unpacking your bags. Richard will welcome you for sure.

Around Chablis

Chablis is a fairly compact village and wine centre that hasn't been transformed into a tourist hotspot despite its rockstar status globally. There is no wine snobbery or exclusivity here but there IS a sense of tradition and pride you can feel around you in shops, bars and brasseries, and with winemakers. Generations of winemakers have developed Chablis into being the best known village for a single grape, the chardonnay, in the world. The village is densely packed with winemakers and surrounded with rolling hills covered in vines, almost acting as a "wall" and not letting you out!

Wine tasting is an arduous activity, especially when visiting Burgundy and particularly in Chablis., Eventually your palate needs a rest, so taking a rest day like the riders on the Tour De France is called for, even though you may be a highly tuned and extremely fit wine tasting athlete! A cultural walkabout is called for, giving you the chance to observe and reflect on the architecture, history and people of this most famous village ...... time for a bit of mindfulness.

There always seems to be a Roman emperor involved when I begin writing a bit of history and this time it's Emperor Domitian who pulled up the vines (!) before winemaking was revived by Emperor Probus from the 5th Century, but there appears to be traces of life here going back to Neolithic times.

Written evidence of Chablis however dates back to 510AD when Sigismond, the first Christian king in Burgundy built a monastery here and then later Charlemagne built the Sainte Marie church. But as usual it was the monks who really developed winemaking for personal drinking but also for shipping to the market of Paris which was accessible from the port of Auxerre via barges. By 1118AD the Cistercian monks of Pontigny Abbey had been granted rights to grow vines over 45 acres of land, and by the mid 15th Century they were shipping wine to Flanders and England too. Around the same time France's 5th Printing House was located in Chablis and the population had risen to a staggering 4000!

Sadly however Chablis got caught up in the religious wars of the early 1600s, when the village was "burned, pillaged and plundered" by the Huguenots. The Huguenots were Calvinistic Protestants who had been granted greater freedoms by Catherine de Medicis which didn't go down well with the Roman Catholic Guise family and the Chablis massacre became known as "Black February" locally. This is probably why a lot of the buildings seem to date from just after this episode. Nevertheless a walk around the village can be done easily in a morning with a picnic lunch maybe above the Grand Cru Les Clos vines where there are a few picnic tables in the woods.

We drove to the picnic area above the grand cru climats which gave us a magnificent view across the entire Chablis landscape and down to the village itself, sparkling in the mid day sun. We'd brought a light picnic lunch of hams, sausages and cheeses with a baguette or two, naturally, but didn't want to overeat because of the special dinner we had planned for tonight. It's from this vantage point that you can get a very good understanding of the classification of Chablis wines based on the "terroir" or total environment in which the vines are growing. You will especially be able to see the slope, aspect and soil involved that makes these wines, and those across Burgundy overall, so special and how the rest of the world is now making wines which are similarly varied and interesting.

A match from the Jurassic era
So, let's begin with a bit of food matching. Across our wine travels we have eaten oysters in Bouzigues, Whitstable, Paris, Rome, Chinon, Glasgow, and all over Brittany, New York, San Francisco and many more. My favourite oyster and wine tasting experiences have been in

Chinon and Glasgow, it is truly an international food that crosses cultural boundaries. There are so many different types of oyster too, from the old native British Oyster to the Russian Tsarskaya Oyster. But ..... what to wash them down with? A wine .... surely? My choice of wine might surprise you but there is a degree of logic about it, because you wouldn't just buy a wine from the region where you are eating the oyster, or a wine/drink related to the oyster's origin. If that were the case it would be Guinness with Irish oysters, vodka with Tsarskaya, Picpoul in Bouzigues, Muscadet in the Loire; all of these work but there's a better choice .... Chablis! So ..... why? It's all to do with the terroir and specifically the soil in which these vines spend their entire lives.

"The Chardonnay vines of Chablis are located in a sedimentary basin. This low-lying zone, once under the ocean, was gradually covered by the material that today make up the soil and subsoil of the Chablis wine region."

So there's the first clue, this region was once under an ocean and the subsoil in Chablis is known as Kimmeridgean, so named after the village of Kimmeridge in Dorset, England.

"The vineyards of Chablis have one sole religion!: the Kimmeridgean," writes Jacques Fanet in his book "Les Terroirs du Vin" published by Hachette. The Kimmeridgean is a geological age in the Upper Jurassic epoch, around 150 million years ago. In Chablis, one finds subsoils of gray marl which alternate with bands of limestone, and sometimes very rich in fossils"

So any guesses what the fossils are? The subsoil is full of Exogyra Virgula, a small, comma-shaped oyster that is characteristic of the marl from the Middle and Upper Kimmeridgean! Now there's a surprise, the Chardonnay grapes of Chablis are growing in and fertilised by oyster shells!

"It is in this very particular subsoil, which in places breaks the surface, that the wines of Chablis draw their unique character, their purity, their sophistication and minerality."

"Ah the oyster, the crazy oyster. These androgynous aphrodisiacs, once the staple diet of poor apprentices, are now the currency for the Gucci-shoed executive who also swallows big deals as he sips a glass of Chablis in the dim blue-suited bars of the capital."

What more could you possibly need to know, the Chardonnay vines are grown in the fossilised shells which are the houses of the oyster you are about to eat! You have 150 million years of evolution and fertilisation advising your wine tasting so don't wait, just do it!

The four grades of Chablis
My first taste of "Chablis" was a wine produced in California or Chile, I'm unsure which one ...... and I am not joking! Back in the 1960s there didn't seem to be any regulation preventing anyone from growing a wine in a particular style and then naming it after that style. I probably drank Spanish Chablis too, but nowadays this all sounds so crazy as to be unbelievable. Today, buy a bottle

of Chablis and you will know where it came from even down to the specific parcel of land where the vines grow.

There are 4 grades or levels of Chablis production: Grand Cru Chablis, Premier Cru Chablis, Chablis, and Petit Chablis. Which level a vineyard is in has nothing to do with the producer or the quality of the wine! It was in 1938 that strict regulations were laid down about which parcels of land were entitled to use the designation Grand Cru based on the soil type and aspect, and there are 7 of them. Premier Cru were next in line to be designated followed by Chablis then lastly Petit Chablis. But of course not all wines are "equal" within a designation and will naturally be affected by the winemaker, equipment, grape yield, etc. This means of course that a wine from a lower designated grouping could be of a higher quality than some wines above it! Naturally this makes for a lot more fun in wine tasting and buying ...... and seeking out the wines from the Chablis and Petit Chablis groupings that are of exceptionally high quality, but don't qualify as Grand or Premier Cru, and are therefore much cheaper. They are not easy to find in your local wine merchants or supermarkets because the buyers for these organisations buy these "better wines" in huge quantities and bump up the price. The way to do it is to visit Chablis itself and tour around lots of small producers over a couple of days. Find the best then fill the boot of your car!

One of the very best sources of consistently high quality and great value Chablis across all four grades is the wine cooperative La Chablisienne in the centre of the village. (I have written about wine cooperatives earlier). The people here are knowledgeable, professional and very friendly, selling all 4 levels of Chablis too. You can taste as much as you like, including the "top of the shop" Grand Cru Grenouille. This is the smallest of the 7 Grand Cru vineyards, but remember there are many different producers holding smaller parcels of land including La Chablisienne and they were on our schedule for a visit tomorrow.

The best Chablis in the world?

Tonight it WAS about the wine, mostly! After much faffing around on my part I had decided to add the Chablis Grand Cru, Les Clos, Domaine Dauvissat onto my wine tasting bucket list. This was after I had discovered that it is cheaper to have a bottle of this particular Chablis in a restaurant in Chablis itself rather than buy it from a wine merchant in England! You couldn't make this up …. The anticipation of tonight's dinner and drinking one particular bottle of wine had become almost suffocating! This was our second day in Chablis and the evening was to be the culmination of much research, planning, communication and organisation ….. crazy …… all for ONE bottle of wine. But not just "any old bottle of wine"!

Domaine Dauvissat and their Chablis Grand Cru, Les Clos are world famous, usually competing with Domaine Raveneau in the minds of professional wine writers as to which one is really the best Chablis on the planet. Margaret Rand in her book "101 Wines to try before you die" had to toss a coin, and it came down Dauvissat. So here we are now in Chablis, walking into Bistro des Grand Crus with a bottle of Dauvissat waiting for us after several rounds of communication with Christian, the restaurant owner, to obtain and reserve a bottle of the 2014 for us. This is Wine #1 on my Wines 101 Bucket List. Once seated, the bottle makes an entrance, carefully tended by Vincent!

The previous day we had tasted 27 different wines as part of our "shopping" so we were finely tuned to the four grades of Chablis, particularly the Premier Cru wines and the Grand Cru Les Clos we had tasted with other producers. As Vincent poured us the first few precious drops the owner came over to "discuss" our initial thoughts …. "hold those thoughts" he said, "they will change within an hour".

Christian was right, our view of the wine changed across the evening, not in terms of enjoyment, but in terms of the sensations of aroma and taste. The wine softened, complexity increased and finish lengthened. Acidity and minerality seemed to decrease too, but this is only our perception of them because the actual "content" of either cannot change.

There are two factors at work here, the exposure of the wine to air, and the combination of sensory inputs from the food with those from the wine, both having a positive effect. I have been reading a lot about this recently, especially regarding the neuroscience of taste and the perception of taste from a philosophical viewpoint. Science plus mind .... as well as cognitive versus sensory inputs, all adding to my understanding and enjoyment of this wonderful hobby. And so the evening came to a close, #1 now tasted, a brilliant wine, but not the end of Wines 101. In two days we would move across to Alsace for #2, and we left the restaurant well satisfied with our hard work! The Dauvissat had definitely met all of our expectations, thanks to a great recommendation from the Wines 101 book and gets our official stamp of approval.

(Finally, we must pay tribute to John Abbot, the owner of a Cambridgeshire inn and restaurant and part time resident of Chablis, who we had befriended via Twitter. We met for the first time on this trip and his advice and help in fixing things was invaluable, so if you're ever in the Cambridge area do visit The Abbots Elm.)

A final tasting or two

Our final day in Chablis before driving up to Ribeauville in Alsace and we had decided on a relatively lazy day with a couple more tastings, then just chilling out sitting in the Cafe La Chablisienne just a stones throw from our hotel. But first we had an early morning tasting fixed by John Abbot who was joining us to introduce us to the winemaker.

The Pinson Family are one of the longest established families in Chablis with records showing them as having been in Chablis since 1640. There is even a Rue Pinson in the village where an earlier generation of three Pinson brothers used to live! The family first started selling its wine in 1880. In 2004 they created a new and state of the art winery, expanding the capacity of it's stock holding, installing a new press house, and also restoring two of its cellars for wines requiring long barrel aging.

Everything is hand-harvested, with sorting of the grapes taking place both in the vineyard and at the winery. Fermentation is mostly in stainless steel using selected yeasts, then the wines are transferred to barrel for the maturation process. The barrels for Grand Cru Les Clos are one to two years old, and for all of their premiers crus three to six years old. The straight Chablis stays in stainless steel.

We arrived at Domaine Pinson, as agreed at 10.30am, and met Corinne Pinson the wife of Laurent, and John Abbot who is the owner of The Abbots Elm and part time Chablis resident. John and I had become friends via Twitter and this was the second tasting he had arranged for me, each being concerned with the Chablis Grand Cru, Les

Clos. I must admit that this was the first time for a few years that I had visited a winemaker for a wine tasting where they didn't speak any English, so we were lucky to have John with us as he speaks French fluently.

As usual we moved through the Pinson grades of Petit Chablis, Chablis, some Premier Crus, and finally the Grand Cru Les Clos. The two lower grades were from 2017 and the two top grades were the 2016 vintage. These were all wines of a VERY high quality, crisp, clean tasting, all in the classic Chablis style and once again I especially liked the Chablis Premier Cru, Fourchaume. I'm really unsure why I am constantly drawn to this climat/plot as this is the fourth winemaker I have bought this particular wine from over the years, including the Cave Cooperative La Chablisienne who first introduced me to it about 10 years ago. My daughter preferred the Chablis Premier Cru Mont de Milieu and we each bought half a dozen of our choices, plus a "few" (!) of the Chablis Grand Cru Les Clos for myself too. Overall, a grand tasting! We'll be back!

Our final tasting was in the early afternoon at the wine cooperative, La Chablisienne, and one we have been coming to for 10 years now and always been warmly welcomed by Sylvie. Expert or novice, ALL are welcomed here and you will find high quality Chablis at good value prices. I had decided not to do any tasting here today as I was looking forward to spending the afternoon in the Cafe La Chablisienne with John and sharing a bottle or two! Sharon and Michael tasted the usual range of wines on offer from Petit Chablis up to Grand Cru before asking my opinion of the Petit Chablis. Here's what I wrote down at the time:

"You really can't buy anything as good as this in a basic Petit Chablis in England. A bargain at around £4.40 for a half bottle, not very complex or such a long finish, but a refreshing glass of light white wine on a hot summers day in the garden"

Sharon bought 24 half-bottles for this bargain price and walked back to the hotel to drive up to the cooperative to load up. It really was a stunning purchase and I wished I had been in my own car or I'd have bought some too, but the boot of Sharon's car was filling up and we now had 3 days of tasting in Alsace. Time to move on!

Chapter 12
2018, Alsace, Ribeauville

"The most curious wine region in France is also one of its most beautiful. The beauty is obvious in the mountain-lined valley with its perfect medieval cobblestone villages, vineyard-lined hills, and half-timber homes. The curiousness is apparent upon meeting the people. Ask producers in the region if they feel more French or more Germanic, and almost all will say French. But it's a peculiar sort of French, as most have a Germanic accent and bearing—stiff, precise, tucked in, intellectual."
(The Sommelier's Atlas of Taste, Rajat Parr & Jordan Mackay)

It was an awkward little journey from Chablis into Alsace and took us 5 hours with a couple of comfort stops. The big BMW was large enough though with plenty of leg room front and back for all four of us. The weather was overcast as we arrived in Ribeauville where we were to spend the next three days in search of #2 on my Wines 101 Bucket List, a grand cru Gewurtztraminer from Domaine Weinbach in the nearby village of Kayserberg. Our hotel was Hotel de La Tour housed in a traditional 17th century building in the town centre, surrounded by restaurants, brasseries and shops so without its own car park. However there is a large public car park behind the hotel and we found a space and began untangling our luggage from all of the cases of wine in the boot which had been packed meticulously like an arrangement of Lego bricks! After checking in we realised how tired we all were and Champa and I decided on an afternoon nap while Sharon and Michael had a wander around choosing a restaurant for dinner later that evening.

A couple of hours later we strolled into the Winstub La Flammerie restaurant which was a 2min walk from our hotel. Lots of dark wooden panels, wooden tables with red tablecloths, and friendly welcoming staff showed us to our table that Sharon had pre booked. We ordered a bottle of Gewürztraminer plus a jug of water and sat back to study the menu having pre warned the two newcomers about mega portion sizes here and pointed out the two giant sized well known dishes of Bacheofe and Choucroute Garni. Michael and I decided to take on the challenge of eating a Bacheofe each, a classic regional dish of "odds and sods" of meat but usually a mix of pork, lamb and thick bacon. These are simmered in wine with onions, leeks, carrots and potatoes in a dough sealed pot for a few hours on a low heat, so probably these had been underway since lunchtime! When they arrived it made the Tarte Flambees ordered by Sharon and Champa look like a snack as we peeled away the dough top from the casserole dish to reveal steaming meat and vegetables in a light coloured gravy. For me it was an effort to finish it but Michael made short work of it! Overall it was a very pleasant evening, good food and great wine with everything being "local", in a setting that was as typical Alsace culture as you can get.

Time for bed, with some serious wine tasting planned for the next two days.

Did I really put a Gewürztraminer on my Wines 101 Bucket List?

Margaret Rand said the following about Gewürztraminer Furstentum, Cuvee Laurence, Domaine Weinbach:

"Gewürztraminer is a bit of a Marmite grape, but at its best it's a great deal more than the face-cream-and-lychees flavours of what the simple examples might suggest. This is Gewürztraminer at its finest. Weinbachs wines are like no other in Alsace. They're extremes, not in the sense of weight, power or showiness, but in their wininess, their minerality. They are sturdy yet elegant, structured but with great finesse."

I have to admit, Alsace wines are not my favourite...... I can appreciate a great wine but I don't necessarily have to like it! But I DO like Alsace the region, especially the strip between Ribeauville and Turckheim.

Wines play a big part of daily life here however: employment, the economy, wine tourism, and culture .... wine dominating the language, relationships, food, history, family ...

But this visit had a very specific wine related purpose, to seek out, taste and buy just one bottle of Gewürztraminer, and more specifically the Grand Cru Furstentum from Domaine Weinbach. This is wine #2 on my Wines 101 Bucket List and I had made an appointment with Catherine Faller, the owner of Domaine Weinbach, to taste this highly rated wine. Unlike Vincent Dauvissat of Chablis .... she agreed to let me in!

We arrived on time at 2.30pm at the Weinbach estate and were welcomed by Theresa, Catherine's assistant, as we entered the hall and were taken through into the classiest tasting room ever! It looked like the drawing room of my grandparent's home from the late 1800s, and I say that with great respect. We loved it as Theresa described the history of winemaking on the estate, the family history and how Catherine became the owner. We began the tasting with a chilled Pinot Blanc, crisp, fresh, slightly acidic and lightly mineral, a good palate cleanser for the "main course".

The Furstentum followed and we were not disappointed, a wine of great complexity, long finish and ... nervosite! We bought two bottles, one for home and one to drink immediately …… But no detailed notes written in situ ….. be patient!

We drove back to our hotel in Ribeauville, got an ice bucket, four glasses and sat outside in the square and opened up the bottle. We sat there for some time, people watching and drinking a bottle of wine that had cost €45, it had a definite citrus and mandarin orange taste, a very "rich and intense wine" that tasted almost sweet, certainly not bone dry, though this sweetness will disappear over time. So, that's #2 done on my Wines 101 Bucket List, not only a different grape, a different wine …. but a different experience in a very classy wine domaine. Now, where should we go next, need to study the book a bit more!

Could YOU taste 270 wines in a single day?

As luck would have it the final two days of our visit coincided with the Ribeauville Annual Wine Festival, honestly this was a coincidence as we had no idea it would be over this particular weekend! I've been to quite a few wine festivals in France but this one took a bit of working out how to get the most from it, and what I describe now took the brain power of all four of us.

The festival was held in and around an area of parkland just outside the main town centre and across the road from the Ribeauville Wine Cooperative. Nothing was free unlike most others I've attended and tickets seemed to be of three types. The lowest price was for a wine glass and the chance to taste 3 wines, the middle price was to taste one wine with a plate of food, and the highest price was to taste three wines with three different small plates of food. I may have that slightly wrong but the gist is correct. Part of the park was set up as an area of "street food" with stalls along one side of the "street" and each stall belonging to a single vigneron/winemaker who was cooking a specific food.

So for example Winemaker X was cooking a spicy prawn and rice dish to match with their Gewurtztraminer and you could hand over your ticket to get a plate of their food and a glass of the matching wine. Now imagine that being repeated down the "street" with each vigneron offering a different food and one of their own wines to match .... quite an interesting concept with 10-15 stalls to choose from.

At the end of this "street" was a large shaded area with bench tables and a large bar set up where you could buy bottles of local wine from a menu or glasses of wine using the appropriate tickets. Live music was being played, French cultural with different bands, and there was a range of other acts for entertainment.

If all of this wasn't enough, something completely different was organised inside a large building on the edge of the park where 270 wines were available for tasting for €8!!! Yes, you read that right, 270!

A large room, with a donut shaped large ring of tasting tables, wine chillers and servers inside the donut. Tasters like myself outside the donut. A catalogue was given with your wine glass and all of the wines were organised by type (fizz, white, red) and by grape (Gewürztraminer, Riesling, Pinot Gris, Pinot Blanc, Muscat, Pinot Noir). Get your Tasting Glass and catalogue, walk around to the numbered station on the donut, tell the waiter the wine # you want to taste, then look, swirl, sniff, taste and .... spit, because 270 is a LOT of wine. I managed 27, daughter and husband got through 40 apiece! Then *zzzzzzz*!

The oldest wine cooperative in France
The previous days marathon tasting had given Sharon and Michael a good idea of the wines they were interested in adding to their own collection, remember that Alsace wines were fairly new to their radar and they had tasted

some really top class Rieslings around that donut! They decided to check out some wines at the Ribeauville wine cooperative and at Domaine Trimbach, the latter being one of the highest rated vigneron in the whole of Alsace.

The Cave de Ribeauvillé is the oldest Wine Coop in France, established in 1895 and has always had a simple philosophy of taking the entire harvest from each member, and paying them fairly, and with only 38 growers everyone involved is serious about creating quality wine. Quality just oozes from the building as soon as you walk inside, as well as the usual tasting bar there are bottles of their most prestigious wines in little alcoves in the walls lit up by yellow lighting. In fact the whole room was lit by I guess what you would call "mood lighting" a gentle yellow that seemed warming and relaxing as well as welcoming. The place is a joy to visit, free tasting of ALL wines, tours of cellars and vines, and exceptional value pricing. Wine Cooperatives are always well worth visiting either as an introduction to wine tasting or as an opening when visiting a region for the first time.

Historically, in 1885 Alsace was annexed to the German Reich, and this was the catalyst for the Cooperative creation. Cut off from France and its wine connoisseurs the vineyards of

Ribeauvillé were sadly neglected and it was a group of winegrowers who then decided to group together. They founded the Ribeauvillé cooperative based on the ideas of German sociologist Frédéric Raiffeisen and initially named it Rappoltsweller Winzerverein. The principle was simple, each member had to bring all his harvest to the cooperative and in exchange was paid fairly. Skilled workers were in charge of the winemaking and bottling, a sales force found outlets for the wine and an administrative body took care of production and selling. Everything was placed under the direct control of the winegrowers who formed a board of directors. A simple principle, but with very clear organisation and comprehensive strategy.

To re-emphasise the quote from above, the vineyards of Ribeauvillé have been here since the beginning of time. But it was the Lords of Ribeaupierre and the Benedictine monks who first recognised the value of its south facing slopes and different topsoils. It is believed that the knight-monk Martin Zahn returning from the Crusades played a major role in the creation of "Clos du Zahnacker". This is their most prestigious plot, a monopole, an enclosed plot which has been the exclusive property of the Cave de Ribeauvillé since 1965. It has a rich history. It has been owned by knights and clergy. As mentioned, it's name comes from one of its first recorded owners, the knight and monk Martin Zahn (Zahn Acker = Zahn's Field). Measuring 1.24 hectare, the Clos du Zahnacker is dominated by the Haut-Kœnigsbourg Castle and is located in the heart of the Grand Cru Osterberg, with a south-east sun exposure. Three grape varieties are cultivated in equal parts among the Clos: Riesling, Pinot Gris and Gewurztraminer all making exceptional wines. Despite all the upheaval in the history of this part of France since 1895, the Cave de Ribeauvillé has survived and stuck to its guiding principle.

I had decided not to buy any wines here myself, as well as not being a big fan of Alsace wines I already had a few in my collection at home and had taken up my fair share of boot space in Sharon's car. But I did go to taste a few and to help Sharon make her choices and find "best value". We tasted mostly Riesling wines from vineyards in different villages and ranging in price from as low as €7 and up to €23 for the special Clos du Zahnacker. Quite often however, a wine "type" to look out for is one labelled vielles vignes (old vines) and means that the particular wine, whatever the grape variety, has been grown on vines of 30-50+ years old with a controlled lower yield and which can result in a wine of greater intensity and complexity. As we tasted our way up the range of Rieslings the one labelled as vielles vignes had a clear "step up" in taste and aroma from the lower priced wines before a bigger step to the grand cru wines. But .... at just €9 per bottle it represented a superb wine without paying €20+ for the grand cru wines. What immediately hit us with this wine was it's aromatic intensity, definitely citrus, still youthful at only 2 years old and would continue to develop for maybe 3-5 years. This was the one to buy and take home, a wine to have at hand in your collection over the next couple of years, to take out of your cellar or chiller either on a warm summer's day in the garden, or at Christmas to go with that foie gras before the turkey! A case of 12 was loaded into the car!

The previous days festival tasting had highlighted the quality of the Riesling wines from the highly acclaimed Maison Trimbach whose winery is in Ribeauville and just a couple of hundred metres away from the cooperative. Founded in 1626 the Domaine is now run by a 12th generation Trimbach, and that takes some beating in wine history terms! I left Sharon and Michael to take the car there to purchase what they had already tasted the day before, they didn't need my help as they knew what they wanted.

And so our combined wine trip in Chablis and Ribeauville drew to a close with wines bought from one of the oldest and most prestigious winemakers in the world. Across these 10 days we had tasted only white wines, three main grapes Chardonnay, Riesling, Gewürztraminer, two of the greatest wines in the world and both on my Wines 101 Bucket List, and found a new personable winemaker in Richard Rottiers at Domaine Les Malandes making high quality Chablis at affordable prices. We'd had great food in both Chablis and Ribeauville though both very different in nature ..... and portion size! One village was very touristy the other more traditional rural French, both were steeped in wine culture so thick and enduring you could taste it, but maybe that's the point, maybe that's why a wine tasted in situ then brought home never tastes quite the same? Is that a physical/physiological effect or one more likely to be psychological/philosophical? Worth thinking about.

Chapter 13
2018, Loire, Fontevraud

"The Loire's great asset is its versatility. Diverse styles abound, from sparkling to sweet and everything in between. Light, mineral-driven whites are a specialty from both ends of the appellation (Muscadet and Sancerre), while medium to heavy-bodied whites can be found in appellations like Vouvray, Montlouis-sur-Loire, and Savenièrres. The reds—whether Pinot Noir or Cabernet Franc, the Loire's two great red specialties—are earthy and dry, medium-bodied at the heaviest, and perfect for today's burgeoning preference for lighter, more versatile red wines."
The Sommelier's Atlas of Taste, Rajat Parr & Jordan Mackay

The most varied of the wine regions we have visited this year, and certainly the biggest ...... a long snaking area from the Atlantic Ocean on the west coast of France almost to Bourgogne and ending around Sancerre. This is the Loire Valley, home to the Cabernet Franc, Chenin Blanc, Sauvignon Blanc and Melon de Bourgogne (!) as the primary grapes of renowned appellations including Savennieres, Chinon, Anjou, Muscadet, Saumur, Vouvray,

Sancerre, Pouilly Fume, Menetou Salon, Saumur Champigny .... an astounding array of grapes, appellations and terroir. Choosing who and where to visit with only 7 days was difficult to say the least.

Choosing to stay in a village near Saumur may not be on every wine tasters radar, but there are wines in this area to knock your socks off including the many Cremant fizz, long lasting Chenin Blanc, as well as Cabernet Franc that gives many a Bordeaux its "something extra". Then there is Saumur-Champigny a serious version of Cabernet Franc. Let's not forget the chateaux, the abbeys, the Plantagenets, Rabelais ..... all within a 10 miles radius, although we did plan to go further afield.

From our Cotswolds home we have two choices of travel across to France, either via a longish drive East into Kent for a short 30mins Eurotunnel journey, or a short 90mins drive South to Portsmouth for a 6-8 hours ferry trip to Caen or Le Havre. It all depends on your ultimate destination in France and this time we intended a holiday near Saumur in the Loire with a short stop at the village of Savennieres for a tasting of some Chenin Blanc, including #3 on my Wines 101 Bucket List. Our arrival at the port of Le Havre after a good sleep on the overnight Brittany Ferries service and subsequent departure for a Savennieres wine tasting was not without incident; returning to our car parked on an outside deck the previous night we discovered we were not to be the first car off the ship but the last, and also that everyone in our lane had to reverse for 30 metres because we'd been parked in a cul de sac! Some 40 minutes later we're off, now only to find that the French gendarmerie have decided to check every car passenger's passports manually! The queue snaked around for about 500 metres, inching forward ….. very slowly. Again, 40 minutes later …. we're off! You don't want to hear about the car satnav throwing a tantrum 30 minutes later and having to switch to dear old Google maps on an iPhone, so I'll just say that 3 hours later, after a ham baguette apiece for lunch, we arrived in the village of Savennières in the Maine-et-Loire department in western France near Anjou. Savennières is the home of Chenin Blanc, the grape used to make long-ageing white wines of outstanding quality and excellent value.

Wines for women!

The Domaine du Closel is one of the top winemakers in the appellation of Savennières and their Clos du Papillon vineyard so highly rated it is on my Wines 101 Bucket List, the next one to be tasted as we spend a week in the Loire Valley. The Clos du Papillon is a butterfly shaped walled vineyard, hence the name. The soil is very shallow here, full of schist, but wines have been made in this land for generations and are mentioned in 1495 in the Chateau des Vaults archives, with its vineyard, orchard and garden. The current chateau, the home of Domaine du Closel, was built in the XVII century and remastered in the XIX century. The park with its current design was created around 1850. The property overall has been in the hands of members of the upper class of Angers and of the prestigious family of Nantes shipowners for centuries and late in the 19th century, the family of Emmanuel de Las Cases, Napoleon's biographer, inherited the estate. Since that day, the Château des Vaults and the vineyards have been managed by the descendants of Las Cases, including Evelyne de Pontbriand the current owner/Manager. How's that for a bit of history to be part of, and Evelyn is a proud traditionalist who is also a keen researcher into "all things Chenin Blanc".

We were met inside the walled entrance area by Adeline who was to be our host for tasting a range of the domaine's white wines. First up was La Jalousie 2015, a fresh example of Chenin Blanc of some minerality, drinking well NOW and a bargain for such quality at €26.90. Next was Les Caillardieres, more closed but with a longer finish and which would peak in 2-5 years. Excellent value at €33.90. Finally, the big one, Les Clos du Papillon 2016, this wine had total Chenin Blanc character, balance, elegance, and would continue developing for another 15 years in bottle. Strong minerality from the schist terroir but balanced with the typical pear/honey notes of this appelation. Definitely a five star scoring wine and well priced at €38.90 which would cost around €50 from a specialist U.K. wine merchant.

Evelyne, the owner, joined us part way through the tasting. She is from a long line of **women** winemakers, first started by Marque de Las Cases du Closel, whose niece, Michèle Bazin de Jessey, developed the vineyard and created the company, Les Vins Domaine Closel, which she has handed down to her two children one of which is Evelyne. As far as I can work out she is the 5th generation of women winemakers here, clearly held in great esteem by her staff and with a wicked sense of humour, and my tongue-in-cheek question of "is this a wine for women" as we tasted the Clos du Papillon had Evelyne laughing her socks off! Naturally I bought plenty too before we continued our journey towards Saumur.

Fontevraud Abbeye

We were staying at the Hotel La Croix Blanche in Fontevraud-l'Abbeye, a village which is situated roughly half way between the "wine towns" of Chinon and Saumur. We had visited the village and Abbey in previous years and had lunch at the hotel as well as just whiling away a sunny afternoon sitting in the comfortable outdoor chairs, wine included naturally! The village is relatively uncommercialised, and except for the daily visitors to the famous Abbey is a peaceful and serene place to stay. The hotel is housed in a 17th Century building in the small square next to the abbey entrance and has comfortable rooms and a good restaurant and bar.

The Abbeye is a stunning building, well preserved, and with a long and interesting history that will appeal to followers of English history too.

"The Abbeye is the largest collection of monastic buildings in all of France - almost a village in itself! Founded in the early 12th century the abbey is set within a perimeter wall which was unfortunately not secure enough to withstand desecration by the Huguenots in the 16th century or partial destruction by the Revolutionaries in the 18th. Napoleon had it converted into a state prison in 1804 and it remained so until 1963 -its most

famous inmate being the writer Jean Genet. Since then it has seen a constant period of restoration removing the damage time had inflicted on it."

When we last visited I was extremely interested to discover that the remains of King Henry II of England, his wife Eleanor of Aquitaine, and his son Richard the Lionheart are entombed here with their effigies in the naive of the abbey church. There is a fourth effigy which I read was the wife of King John, Richard's brother, the king who signed the Magna Carta. His wife? Where the heck was John? Well, a quick tap on my iPhone revealed that John was buried in Worcester Cathedral in 1216, but the question remained as to why he wasn't buried here with his effigy next to his mother and father. So, on leaving after our visit I spoke to one of the curators who gave me an extensive and enlightening answer. Apparently while Johns body was entombed in Worcester, his heart was placed in a gold casket and entombed with his wife at Fontevraud. However during the French Revolution vandals sacked the abbey and, knowing that a gold casket was there, they stole it! Myth or true? No idea, and I haven't yet found that explanation anywhere else!

Wife snaps while I drink wine!
Wine tasting my way through a Wines 101 Bucket List

had become an exercise in logistics, decision making, communication and relationship building! I naively thought that the reclusive nature of old world winemakers in France had disappeared, but it hasn't, far from it as I discovered in Chablis, and now in Chinon. I have no intention of naming names because I totally respect a winemaker who just wants to care for his vines, make his wine, then sell it to his preferred clients. No visits, no tastings, no purchases, no phone, no website. But in such cases how do they EVER get into a book that recommends the 101 wines you should try before you die? In some cases so far, as I've said before I'd die before they answered their bloody phones or sold me a bottle!

My solution? Buy another book, 1001 Wines to Buy Before You Die! No, I am not chasing 1001 wines, I am seeking recommended substitutes if a wine from Wines 101 isn't available to me, and this was the case in Chinon, a town and area we love in France and have visited many times over the past 35 years.

We drove into Chinon and parked at Clos de L'Echo, a vineyard owned by Domaine Couly-Dutheil within sight of Chateau Chinon. It was once owned by the family of Rabelais, the French renaissance writer, monk, and humanist, whose name gave rise to the expression Rabelaisian meaning "earthy humour, bawdy"! In my opinion, the Cabernet Franc wines of this area are certainly earthy.

The tasting room is a small building amongst the L'Echo vines which is as authentic an environment as it gets. A welcoming cool environment inside with the temperature already approaching 30 degrees by mid day, as we were met by Myriam who would host our tasting. I only tasted two vintages of the Clos de L'Echo, 2015 & 2014. The earlier vintage had the classic Cabernet Franc aromas and taste, typical earthy tones and moderate to high tannins. In discussion with Myriam we thought that this great wine would age for some 10-15 years. The 2015 was quite different, moderate tannins, but much lighter in intensity and length of finish making it easy drinking now. I bought a case of the latter as I though that the former might outlast me at my age! Anyway, that's another Wines 101 in the cellar!

Meanwhile Champa started to pursue her own new hobby, photographing with her iPhone anything that wasn't a bottle of wine or that involved me drinking wine! So, as I'm engaged in "fascinating conversations" about minerality and apogee, she wanders off snapping vines, leaves, grapes, barrels, tanks, wall art.

We left the car parked outside Clos de L'Echo and wandered down into the town centre of Chinon via the lift near the Chateau (store that fact away for useful reference!) for a light lunch at the A la Pause Rabelaisienne brasserie. It seemed fitting after visiting a vineyard once owned by the Rabelais family!

"Loire Valley wines have forever been mainstays in blind tasting flights for young sommeliers. After all, the Loire is a classic, a true standard of French wine as stated by the textbooks we all studied as we fell under the seductive spell of wine. But, going back just ten years ago, even if Loire reds and whites made frequent appearances in blind tastings, they rarely received much

attention beyond that (excepting Sancerre). That is, we tasted them and studied them, but didn't really drink them. Of course, all that has changed now, and dramatically so. Today, we drink them lustily."

The Sommelier's Atlas of Taste, Rajat Parr & Jordan Mackay

Two chateaux, no wine tasting
1. Chateau de Montreuil-Bellay

Don't you just love French Chateau, especially if they are involved in winemaking too! Externally preserved quite wonderfully because Oliver Cromwell and his cannons had no cause to cross the water, but often bereft internally, stripped of all furnishings. A marvellous exterior is often let down by a soulless interior. But, our plan for this third day was to visit two chateaux each within an easy drive from our hotel.

We visited the small town of Montreuil-Bellay first with its fantastic chateau giving a chance for my palate to recuperate from the battering it had taken over the first two days of our Loire holiday. We had no intention of going inside because this Chateau only permitted guided visits ..... and in French, no self guided/wandering visits! Still worth a trip though, only 5 miles away from our hotel at Fontevraud. Here's a little background on the place.

"The town of Montreuil-Bellay retains almost all of its medieval walls, making it one of the last fortified towns of the Anjou region. It is well worth a visit as it still retains its medieval feel. Its strategic location on the borders of Anjou, Touraine and Poitou allowed the town to grow and have an important regional administrative function (subsequently transferred to Saumur) before the French Revolution, this accounts for the number of fine houses in the town".

"During the French Revolution the castle was seized by the revolutionary government and used as a prison for women suspected of being royalists. In 1860 the daughter of Saumur businessman Adrien Niveleau, (who had bought it in 1822) undertook occupancy and set about a major restoration campaign, redoing some of the rooms in the Troubadour style. Descendants of her husband's nephew are the current owners of the property."

"Château Montreuil-Bellay is also the name of fine wines of the area produced from vines within the chateau grounds. The grapes, apparently harvested and sorted by hand, are made into wine in the fifteenth-century wine cellars."

We didn't have a tasting here (honest!) but did inspect the charming wine tasting room that also served as a reception and ticket office. The chateau had quite a presence to it with its drawbridge entrance, massively thick walls and classic pointed turrets so common of not only this area but the whole of the Loire. Parts of the chateau date back to the year 1025 and earlier, but much of the development of what you see occurred in the 1500s with internal refurbishment taking place in the 1860s. Situated above the banks of the River Thouet the village of

Montreuil-Bellay was once an important site for the transportation of wine, and it's a pleasant though somewhat hilly area to meander down to the river and take a quite wide circular walk around the chateau itself. It took us about an hour with magnificent views of the chateau from all angles, before returning to La Barbacane brasserie directly opposite the chateau entrance. A simple omelette and a glass of the local wine set yours truly up for a second cultural visit for the afternoon!

2. Chateau de Breze

It's only a few miles drive from Montreuil-Bellay to Breze and we drove through the beautiful village of Breze just 15 minutes later. Parking alongside the Chateau prompted different emotions, Champa was delighted because we were surrounded by vines she could explore and snap away at, with myself experiencing the usual wave of scepticism regarding a glorious exterior that was probably devoid of artefacts or any sense of culture and history within those gleaming walls.

Having paid my €9 entrance fee I was one of the few people entering after lunchtime through the central gate in the walls, having crossed a wooden bridge over a heck of a chasm that was probably once a moat, though it looked very natural. In the main courtyard the guidebook told me to enter Door #1, logically, as this would take me into various tunnels before exiting outside in between the chateau walls and some sort of exterior walls in the tuffeau. This is local limestone in The Loire Valley and often burrowed into by troglodyte cave dwellers. (More on this later when we visit the Domaine Filliatreau in Saumur-Champigny)

I emerged from these tunnels and was immediately astounded at my surroundings, I had entered a doorway in the main courtyard, wandered around a maze of non-descript tunnels, and arrived blinking into the sunlight at the bottom of the moat! This outer wall of the moat or cliff face surrounding the main chateau walls was riddled with "caves/holes" like a Swiss cheese, but I instinctively knew they would have a purpose, and so it proved. Kitchens, a bakery, storage rooms and …. caves related to wine making with the original artefacts still in situ. I wandered through many of these caves for about an hour, marvelling at the size and construction of grape presses, fermenting vats and barrels, almost certainly all constructed in oak. Massive alcoves had been dug out within each cave to house each piece of equipment and I could only imagine the sweat and toil of the people who created them, the craftsmen who had built the presses and lowered them into the bottom of the moat. Then there was surely the problem of getting the wine the 100metres or so to the top of the moat up to ground level for transport and trade. Meanwhile in adjacent caves there would have been peasant serfs working in the kitchens baking bread, roasting meats, preparing stews day after day to keep the aristocratic owners of the castle in the luxury to which they were accustomed.

I really enjoyed this visit, discovering the wine equipment in the caves was a big surprise because my prior research had been minimal to say the least. I was lucky, we could have missed seeing this chateau situated only a few miles away from our hotel in Fontevraud! Sadly the main interior was most disappointing, as usual, with no-entry signs everywhere. But, if only the walls could talk ….

Footnotes

"Built between the 11th and 19th centuries in the heart of a vineyard with an area of several dozen hectares, the castle of Brézé has belonged to the powerful and influential family of the Dreux-Brézé for centuries, before being taken over – by marriage – by the family of Colbert, descendant of the Minister of Louis XIV. The castle of Brézé reflects a rich history dating back to at least the mid-fifteenth century, during which the castle was fortified. It was in fact the subject of numerous construction plans and alterations to its architecture.

In addition to the underground tunnels, the dry moats are an impressive sight and are considered among the deepest in Europe. A visit to the castle will also be the opportunity to discover the largest known underground medieval bakeries in France, with its imposing fireplace and chimney. Walking along the moats, you will pass by three wine presses of the sixteenth century. The presses, still working, are part of the largest currently known in the west of France. Beautiful tools used to produce the wine are still found here too."

No cats pee or gooseberry bush thank you!

If you're a lover of Sauvignon Blanc you will probably already have your favourites, New Zealand or Chile, branded or labelled by the grape ….. or maybe Sancerre from France which immediately tells you something about the terroir and culture behind the wine. The problem is that Sauvignon lovers are often hit in the pocket for buying such a wine from Sancerre, especially if in a restaurant, so what to do? My advice as always, step outside the region of interest, Sancerre in this case, it's only a geographical boundary. Just like delineated wine villages such as Meursault…… expensive, or …… St Aubin ….. cheaper and still in Burgundy, same soil, same grape, …… and just next door.

Next to Sancerre is Menetou-Salon, a smaller district of unlimited potential with Domaine Pelle leading the way, and I knew this because I had bought some of their wines from The Wine Society (UK) and enjoyed them immensely. Also, one of their wines was now on my Wines 101 Bucket list and we were on holiday in the Loire Valley just a 3 hours drive away from Domaine Pelle …… too good an opportunity to miss!

Located directly southwest of Sancerre, this relatively small appellation produces a brilliant range of high-quality white, red and rosé wines that offer excellent value.

Sauvignon Blanc is the predominant grape here with some Pinot Noir now being cultivated too. The vines are mostly planted in upper Jurassic Kimmeridgian limestone sediment, exactly the same as in Chablis, and the wine style is definitely terroir driven.

The appellation covers an area of 10 communes, one of which is Menetou-Salon itself. Menetou-Salon is an ancient wine-producing area if old writings and documents about the lordship of Menetou are to be believed. Documents from the years 1063, 1097 and 1100 have been recovered, where the Lord of Menetou gave a donation to different religious orders in the region, most particularly to the Saint-Sulpice-lès-Bourges Abbey, with vines located close to Davet.

We had chosen to visit the Domaine Henry Pelle and had written to the owner, Anne Pelle, about a visit from our base for the week near Saumur, a 3 hour drive away. Their Vignes de Ratier was on my Wines 101 Bucket List and I was keen to add it to my other wine from this Domaine I had bought previously from The Wine Society (UK).

We were met and hosted by Serge before Anne arrived, and he gave us a quick tour around the winery before lining up 8 wines to taste; three red Pinot Noir and 5 white Sauvignon Blanc.

The Pinot Noir were deep red in colour, much more so than Volnay and Pommard from the same grape. In aroma and taste they were similar to Irancy which is at the extreme northern end of Burgundy and between Sancerre and Chablis so most similar in overall terroir including the climate.

The white wines, all from Sauvignon Blanc, were absolutely typical of the Sancerre style and completely devoid of the regular gooseberry and cats pee aromas. These aromas are a bi product of yeasts and fermentation and certainly put a lot of people off Sauvignon Blanc based wines, though they are a natural presence. I decided to buy a couple of cases of each, a bargain at €18 and €14 for each bottle of red and white respectively.

When Anne joined us she seemed genuinely pleased that a member of The Wine Society had travelled so, far to visit their winery and taste their wines. She told me that The Wine Society was their first big client and that their association goes back around 40 years. If that isn't an endorsement of quality, I don't know what is! And .... another on my Wines 101 Bucket List ticked off. We drove back to Fontevraud well pleased and ready for a big day out on the final day of our holiday tomorrow.

Footnote

Paul-Henry Pelle was born in 1985. He was raised in Morogues – like his great-grandfather, grandfather and father, and just like them, he chose to become a wine grower. He did his training at the lycée viticole in Beaune and through internships with Olivier Lamy in St-Aubin and Benjamin Leroux at Clos des Epeneaux. With the first of these, he learned how to appreciate the distinct

identity of each terroir and the appropriate use of the different
containers (vats, barrels, etc.) in the winery; with the second, he
learned the importance of ploughing the soils to respect the plant.
The wine estate's first vintages were 2006 and 2007, crafted
under the expert eye of Julien Zernott, who has overseen the
winemaking process since 1995.

In 2007, aged 22, Paul-Henry took charge of the vineyards and
the winery, accompanied by Anne (his mother) who has managed
the office since the end of the 1980's. Following on from three
generations who created, established and perpetuated the wine
estate, he is guiding it towards finesse and consistent quality.

Since his return, the progressive work in the vineyards and the
winery has resulted in the production of "precise" wines with
each vintage. Each bottle represents the terroir and year that
brought it to fruition. His aim – the simple expression of the
terroir.

Wine, Seafood and a Chateau in Saumur

Our final day, and one that required quite a bit of planning
and scheduling if everything was to be packed in. After
breakfast we kicked off by making a phone call to Le
Grand Bleu, the amazing seafood restaurant in Saumur, a
long time favourite of our whole family, before driving into
Saumur and up to visit the chateau. Our first and only visit
to the chateau had been almost 30 years ago, and never to
be forgotten! It was memorable in the same way that you
develop an aversion to broccoli, brussels sprouts and
cheese pie from school dinners in the 1960s! I suppose this
needs explaining, but basically it was the first time we had
paid as a family with two young children for a tour of
Chateau de Saumur with a guide who only spoke French.
This was OK because we reasoned that we would have

plenty to look at inside which would be self explanatory. However all of the rooms were empty, vacuous, devoid of ….. well, anything really, not a stick of furniture, nor a tapestry or carpet or painting! And so developed our family aversion to French chateau.

So there you have it, French Chateau, love 'em on the outside, hate 'em on the inside! Soulless, bereft of character, mostly empty or with a few artefacts as an afterthought! But, we love French Chateau, so don't misinterpret my comparison, if only they would do some recreation work their appeal would be even greater.

The Chateau de Saumur

"Standing on top of a rocky outcrop, the Château of Saumur proudly overlooks the surrounding town and its imposing silhouette can be seen from beyond the river. A magnificent testimony to princely residences under the Valois dynasty, the château could almost have been plucked from a fairy tale."

"The first stones were laid in the 10th century by Theobold the Trickster, Count of Blois. It was not long, however, before the château was seized by the impetuous Fulk III the Black who made it the property of the counts of Anjou. It later fell into the hands of the Plantagenets before being won back for the French throne

by Phillip Augustus of France in 1203. At this time, four towers were built around the keep, which served as a basis for the current château. In the 14th century, Louis I of Anjou received the château as appanage and transformed it into a magnificent princely residence, as illustrated in the famous Très riches heures du duc de Berry miniatures. New accommodation was built and the towers and outer walls were raised, complementing the height of the chimneys, gables and belvederes. During the reign of Good King René, the château underwent further restoration work when the chapel was rebuilt, complete with a private oratory. The prince and poet embellished the interior to receive the French Court in the sumptuousness he loved to embody. After the king's death, the Château of Saumur was somewhat forgotten for around a century until the town was ceded to the Protestants."

At the time of our visit the town was pursuing relentless renovation work to restore the château to the splendour as in **Très Riches Heures du Duc de Berry**, a French Gothic manuscript illumination which is really a "book of hours" from the 15th Century. Recently the gilded finial at the top of the south tower was replaced by an exact replica of the one in the legendary Illumination.

Externally Saumur Chateau is a magnificent sight whether you are down below in the town or up close among the vines. But this is where I always hesitate in France, to go in or not to go in, will I learn anything, will I discover something new, will I be awestruck by a magnificent interior depicting life in the Chateau from a bygone age? So, ignoring a previous disappointment from almost 30 years ago I left Champa sitting in the shade of the cafe in the vines, paid my fee, and entered. First impressions of the courtyard and views down to the town and Loire extremely favourable ….. but ….. I wasn't inside yet! Sadly for me, it was all downhill from now on, nothing to really excite me. An old winding mechanism of some sort by the entrance, then a series of rooms with several wall hangings, each room holding collections of various pottery pieces from a variety of places and styles. NOT what I expected inside such a magnificent building. But I guess it mirrors a similar chateau at Montsoreau nearby which is now stuffed as a museum of modern art! Never mind, there was now an awesome Grand Plateau of seafood to look forward to!

A seafood lunch

We drove down from the chateau to a large car park situated just before the Pont Cessart and alongside the D947. It's called Parking Moliere and convenient because its a short walk from here to the centre of Saumur and many restaurants and brasseries. It's also useful to know that you do NOT have to pay for parking in France between 12.00 and 15.00, they take their lunches VERY seriously! We walked down a couple of narrow streets with an eclectic mix of shops and into Le Grand Bleu to be seated at our chosen table inside and out of the searing heat which was now close to 30 degrees C! We knew what we wanted so it didn't take long to check the menu and choose the very large seafood platter to share, piled high with oysters, moules, palourdes, tellines, large prawns and with a flipping big crab on top! Served with a cold glass of chenin blanc house wine and plenty of baguette. I look back on this seafood platter with more than a little nostalgia because it was the last one I ever ate! A few short months later I was diagnosed as a Coeliac meaning I was completely gluten intolerant so no more bread. But what was totally bizarre was the onset of an intolerance of shellfish too. Thank goodness there is no intolerance of grapes! Anyway I cannot recommend this restaurant highly enough, pure class, not cheap, but if you love seafood and visit Saumur …….. Just do it!

Wine tasting with troglodytes ….. No pressure!

The French wine appellation of Saumur-Champigny has been missing off my radar for at least 30 years, and I know this because it was 1987 when my last wine log record shows I drank a bottle! At that time I was mostly buying and drinking "well aged clarets" (red Bordeaux wines) so the lighter style of the Cabernet Franc based wines of this area probably didn't appeal.

Times and tastes change, especially with age, and this visit to the Loire Valley was a good chance to try again, especially since I now rarely buy clarets and favour the lighter style wines from Pinot Noir and Gamay. Our base at Fontevraud situated between Chinon and Saumur, so visiting the small Saumur-Champigny area was a simple with Domaine Filliatreau located in the village of _ ant. This is an area of tuffeau, the limestone rock famous for housing troglodyte dwellers in their caves created in the rock itself and the Filliatreau tasting venue is inside a tuffeau cave. However it's the tuffeau rock and soil that gives the wines here their unique character:

"The terroir around Champigny is vital to the production of wines in this style and is the reason the area was singled out for its own independent appellation. A low plateau of tuffeau – the yellowish metamorphic rock so distinctive of the central Loire region – rises up at the eastern edge of Saumur town and continues almost uninterrupted for seven miles (11km) to the village of Candes Saint-Martin. This sandy, porous rock is the key to much of the Saumur wine character; it regulates water supply to the vines by immediately absorbing excess water and retaining it for use in the driest periods. Vines growing in tuffeau-rich soils rarely suffer from excess water stress but also benefit from dry, free-draining soils."

The wines of Saumur-Champigny are predominantly made from Cabernet Franc, and are typically lighter in style, with fresh acidity and spicy flavours of red berries and violets and best drunk within five to 10 years of bottling. So onwards to the tasting!

Our host was Charlotte who was welcoming, friendly, knowledgeable and …. generous with her pouring! She lined up 6 different vintages and styles from the domaine and explained each one in terms of the terroir and each years weather. Each was light with balanced acidity and tannin, fruity in most cases with red berries and hints of violets as expected, though the 2005 vintage was less tannic and more earthy, also as expected. At this point Charlotte took out another bottle but hid the label from me as she poured me a glass and asked me to guess the vintage!

A generous portion was poured into my glass and Charlotte then stood back, gestured at the glass and smiled! The two other visitors to my left stopped tasting and watched …. no pressure then! Champa looked sideways at me and nodded, that was the only encouragement I needed, except for a little help from my philosophy "friends" Sartre, Heidegger and existentialist thinking! I swirled the wine around the glass and held it over a clean white page of my notebook, a definite brown tinge at the meniscus and certainly less garnet in colour, darker in fact. So, this wine is NOT of a recent vintage, say 2015-2017. My initial swirl and sniff revealed a definite earthiness I always get with Cabernet Franc which also seems to increase with age. The first taste was a surprise, softened tannin but still some acidity confused my taste buds to hell, or was it the other way round? The wine revealed more fruit and floral notes than the 2005 I had tasted earlier, so my brain told me that this is younger than 2005, could it be a 2010 which was a high scoring vintage for the region, or a 2009, also a brilliant harvest year with vintages either side of 2009/10 being less good? I told Charlotte I had narrowed it down to 2 years, she smiled again and told me to choose ..... I went for the 2010 based purely on knowledge of other wines from Chinon I had bought in 2015. "Well done" she said turning the bottle around to reveal a 2010 label and astounding the audience to my left who just said "how the hell did you do that?"." Charlotte explained it to them, I was too exhausted!

Domaine Filliatreau is a lovely vigneron to visit for an informative tasting of wines that are easy to drink. It's in an unusual setting within a tuffeau cliff face, vines to the front, all of which adds to the overall experience. The wines are well priced and excellent value whether you want immediate drinking or something that will mature over a few years. I bought a case of Grand Vignole 2017 for €11 per bottle, drinking well now to which I gave a score of 4 stars on my 5 star scale.

It was a good way to end a great week in the Loire!

Chapter 14
2018, Burgundy, Chablis & Beaune

"Burgundy—the spiritual home of terroir, the mecca of minutia—is where wine asks you if you're ready to take the next step in your relationship. Do you really love me? Are you just a drinker, looking no further than your next glass? Or are you serious, ready to ask questions and listen, ready to study topographical maps and memorize vineyard names? What's your commitment?"
The Sommelier's Atlas of Taste, Rajat Parr & Jordan Mackay

Being retired and with a decent level of pensions and investments gives you a freedom that some of us dream of, but also a state that some of us planned for since student days. Time on our hands, no debt, surplus monthly income ...... all sweated and strived for over 40 years, and these were some of the thoughts and the driving force for another wine trip one miserable wet November day in 2018. We'd had some great holidays across the year including a cruise, long weekend tours of our own country, two wine trips to France, and it was the weather and a little boredom made us decide to take a very short notice late year break to dear old Burgundy again. Within 24 hours we had booked a hotel for a single night in Reims, a return Eurotunnel journey, hotels in Chablis and Beaune for a couple of nights each, and a single night in Epernay in the Champagne region.

We did some rapid research and came up with some things to do that did NOT focus on wine tasting, but which DID have a historical connection to wines that we thought would be interesting and not too crowded at this time of the year. We planned ahead and booked dinner at our favourite restaurant in Chablis and emailed our friends at Domaine Michel Rebourgeon in Pommard to inform them of our visit and inviting them out for dinner for when we arrived in Beaune.

After an early morning start from our Cotswolds home we caught the Eurotunnel 10.50am departure and arrived on the outskirts of Reims as it was getting dark and checked in at the Qualys Hotel Reims, Tinqueux. We were quite hungry after such a long days driving and having looked around the "industrial" area surrounding our hotel found a Chinese restaurant serving one of those all-you-can-eat buffets for €12! Not our usual style when visiting France and it was quite an effort reading a menu of Chinese food written in French and eventually we gave up and just started helping ourselves from the dozens of dishes ……… meat, fish, vegetables, rices, noodles in heated stainless steel vats in a long row you could walk around. I remember doing this when we were students and the memory was triggered as we observed lots of young people in small groups eating enough food that would have kept us both going for a week, and trying not to laugh. Naturally we didn't have any wine with the meal, but it was enjoyable as an experience and set us up for a good nights sleep before driving on to Chablis the next day.

Chablis

Its just over 2.5 hours drive from Reims to Chablis and we arrived early afternoon at our hotel having had a late and filling breakfast. The journey brings you into Chablis from the North East via Tonnere and finally through and alongside the Grand Cru and Premier Cru vineyards.

It was now late Autumn and the view was absolutely magnificent with the leaves still on the vines, a golden carpet in the clear blue sky stretching for miles before us and down into the village itself. I can't remember visiting around here at this time of year, that period between the leaves being green and hiding the fruit, and the leaves being completely absent when all you can see is row after row of the wood of the vines.

We checked in at the Hostellerie de Clos, our favourite hotel in Chablis which had been fully booked the last time we visited here in July which had disastrous consequences with us staying in a relatively unpleasant hotel in the centre of the village. The Hostellerie owns and is next door to the Bistrot des Grand Cru where we had enjoyed the first of my Wines 101 Grand Cru Chablis, also in July, and we had booked a table with Christien for tomorrow evening. It was a good decision and we were to have a very entertaining and unusual evening there too! We had no specific plans for today and spent some time just wandering around the village, it was very quiet with very few tourists around, and we walked along the Serein river footpath from our hotel and back into the centre then sat for a while in the Cafe La Chablisienne surrounded by locals all of who nodded at us and said "bonjour" as if they knew us or remembered us, which I doubt very much. Later that evening we had dinner at the Les Trois Bourgeons, a small restaurant in the centre of the village and described in the Michelin Guide as follows:

"This contemporary bistro, with its understated decoration, has blossomed within the walls of an old cellar of famous Chablis producer Domaine Laroche. A Japanese team, trained in some of the top French houses, treats its customers to fine cuisine inspired by the region's repertoire, and revisited with taste and imagination. Very good value for money."

This is a very "cosy" restaurant with only 6-8 tables and with an open style kitchen where you can see everything the chefs are doing. Prices are reasonable for this quality of food and there is an extensive wine list, mostly Chablis of course and quite rightly. What else would you drink with a plate of oysters followed by a dorade in a white sauce with asparagus? We walked back to our hotel in the cool late evening with the streets virtually deserted, just how we like it!

The biggest wine decanter in the world

The next morning got off with a bang at breakfast as Champa set fire to the "pancake warmer" triggering the hotel fire alarms. It was no big deal and gave everyone a laugh. We had a packed day ahead of us before we headed for Beaune tomorrow, including a visit to a museum, a walk between the Grand Cru vines, and a very interesting dinner and exchange with a group of Germans!

We'd had a very pleasant surprise on reading about The "Treasure of Vix" a few days before our visit here, discovering that the museum housing the Treasure was less than an hours drive away from Chablis. The Treasure is a collection of artefacts housed in the Vix Museum at Chatillon-Sur-Seine, and being situated between the end of Champagne and beginning of the Burgundy regions of France so it really was a no-brainer for us to spend a couple of hours visiting!

The opening lines of the museum brochure invite you in with a promise of seeing something spectacular and unparalleled from the Iron Age:

"25 centuries ago, a lavishly dressed princess is buried at the bottom of Mount Lassois. Discovered in 1953, the most prestigious princely burial from the end of the first Iron Age (500 BC) reveals a lady lying on a chariot and adorned with precious jewels including a gold torque, a masterpiece of Celtic craftsmanship. By her side, the famous bronze vase 1.64 metres in height, a unique and powerful reference of Greek art."

There are four floors to the museum and several collections each representative of a different aspect of life across the ages in The Pays Chatillonnais including The Gallo Roman,

Religious Art, Ornithology, Marshall Marmont Empire and Industry. It was the Gallo Roman we decided to focus on, saving the Marshall Marmont section, especially loads on local ironmaking, for another time.

We arrived in Chatillon on Armistice Day with crowds of observers breaking up and wandering through the town on their way home, and we parked in a large public car park opposite the museum. The museum building is the restored Notre Dame Abbey, founded by St Bernard of Clairvaux in the 12th Century and also having become a hospital after The French Revolution. Like most museums of this type it's an imposing and interesting building in its own right and you get the feeling of wealth and power as you walk between the large pillars and into the central quadrangle towards the entrance door.

Having paid our entrance fee of a very reasonable €7 each, we immediately took the lift up a couple of levels to that housing The Vix Crater, the large bronze vase used as a wine vessel which is probably the largest wine decanter on the planet and holding around 1000 litres of wine. Thirsty beggars these Gauls!

"The bronze crater/vase was produced by a Laconian (from

Sparta) colony in Southern Italy and weighing 208 kg is the largest bronze Greek vessel preserved to this day. On the handles are two Gorgons with a frieze of chariots and warriors between them. It also has a lid/strainer, topped by a statuette of a young girl, and probably acting as a filter any liquid poured into it."

Mont Lassois is an isolated hill overlooking the Seine valley just 6 kilometres from Chatillon. It was occupied from the Neolithic period but with a peak during the Iron Age as a site along the "tin route" transporting the metal from Cornwall in Britain and I had a keen interest in this because my maternal grandparents and beyond were tin miners from Cornwall. Around this entire area thousands of archeological sites have been excavated leading to the discovery of hundreds of tombs in the classic dome shaped tumulus. Especially of some significance was the Vix tomb as it is an example of a Wagon Tomb in which the body of the deceased was placed in a wagon facing forwards, the wagon being a symbol of the sun and the life cycle.

The range of artefacts in the museum from this area is extremely varied ranging from bronze urns and bowls to clay pots, from pins and clasps to statues and skeletons. We hope you will be inspired to visit this museum not too far off the A26 Autoroute south of Reims, it surely shows that Roman propaganda was definitely at work branding the Gauls as Barbarians! Remember too that what I am writing here refers only to the Gallo-Roman artefacts and history, worth a couple of hours on their own, but there is lots to explore about Ironmaking in the area and the huge industrial landscape that used to dominate the scene.

Now, I freely admit that I was initially attracted to this museum because I wanted to see "the largest wine decanter in the world", but my interest and enjoyment grew as we made further discoveries about the people who commissioned and made the decanter, together with their history and culture within a region that today is sandwiched between two of the greatest and best known wine regions in the world, Champagne and Burgundy. A coincidence? I think not!

The Cheval Blanc

This is the latest time of the year we have visited Chablis, just a couple of days to visit a few winemakers before moving on to Beaune further south for a week. From a landscape photography viewpoint the timing was perfect, the leaves of the Chardonnay vines all ready to fall and creating a golden hue as far as the eye could see, so we fancied a bit of a walk right up to the vines along the D965. It's an easy walk from the village centre, over the River Serein and along the Avenue d'Oberwesel passing several famed vigneron Simonnet Febvre, William Fevre Oberwesel, and Christian Moreau before turning left to look up at the grand cru vineyards now on our right.

All wine here is made from the Chardonnay grape and classified into 4 Appellation or "grades". These appellation/grades are awarded to areas of land, not to wines or to winemakers, and are based on the soil composition, the slope and aspect of the area, or more simply the field. Each "field" is sub divided into parcels of land being owned by many different winemakers. The top fields are graded as Grand Cru Chablis, then there are a series of fields graded as Premier Cru Chablis, followed by the "Village" fields just known as Chablis, and lastly the lowest grade fields known as Petit Chablis.

We are now walking alongside the 7 climats/fields (areas of land) graded as Grand Cru Chablis and they are named as Blanchot, Bougros, Les Clos, Grenouille, Le Preuses, Valmur and Vaudesir. I have a single favourites here, Les Clos, but what now enters into the fray of buying any of this Grand Cru wine is ...... who owns a parcel of land in each climat and makes the wine to MY taste. There are lots to choose from and this is part of the fun of visiting a French wine region, choosing a grade/field, then wandering around and tasting different winemakers efforts!

Looking up at the slopes of Les Clos, the Grand Cru climat, we could see a white horse slowly plodding between the vines.

We stopped to investigate and met Arnaud who has two such horses and works for a number of clients who use a completely organic approach to their winemaking. This involves ploughing between the vines without tractors, avoiding the use of pesticides and fungicides or anything that is chemical instead of natural, and in some cases working the land according to the phases of the moon. With the latter this would be a fully "biodynamique" approach.

We chatted to Arnaud for some time and he told us that he

has five client winemakers in Chablis, including Richard Rottiers from Domaine Les Malandes who is one of our favourites and it is Richard's parcel that Arnaud is ploughing. A few hours later, to round off the day in this small but world famous wine village, we were having dinner in Bistrot des Grand Crus and when we entered later that evening, I told Christian, the owner, that we'd met a man with a big white horse earlier to which he said "Oh that must be Arnaud, he lives next door to me"!

In vino veritas et amicitia

This evening we were having dinner at Bistrot des Grands Crus, just a few metres away from our hotel. You will recall from an earlier chapter that we had last been here a couple of months ago as we sought out the first wine on my Wines 101 Bucket List, a Dauvissat Grand Cru, Les Clos and we hope you find this evenings tale interesting and maybe even stimulating as it reiterates the title of this book and our oft used expression "it's not about the wine!"

We were welcomed on entering by Christian, the owner/manager, who led us towards our previous table which was already occupied, so he sat us at the one next to it. We chatted for a few minutes about our previous visit and the very special wine he had obtained for us before he described the daily specials. I ordered a seafood salad as starter, Dr C ordered a squash soup, and we both followed with a trout in an almond sauce. I chose a small carafe of Petit Chablis to accompany which arrived in short order.

The table next to us was occupied by 3 men, one of whom leaned across to me and asked me about the Dauvissat Chablis Premier Cru he had heard Christian and I talking about from the earlier visit. I told him of my Wines 101 quest and that it undoubtedly was the best Chablis I had ever tasted in my long life and what a treat it was to share it with family too. They had chosen a bottle of Fèvre Premier Cru, Vaulorent, and he, without hesitation, poured me half a glass to taste! They introduced themselves as one master sommelier, a colleague and a business owner from Germany who were visiting Chablis then Meursault for tasting and purchasing pallet loads of wine for import into Albert Kierdorf's wine business. Albert was the one who poured me the Fèvre!

Albert now called Christian over and asked him for a bottle of the Dauvissat I had previously bought, only to be told that there was none left. Albert asked him if he had any other Dauvissat, and Christian replied "yes, a 2014 Premier Cru Vaillons, but it's not ready yet so I really couldn't sell it"! Oh dear, I thought WWIII was imminent until Albert explained they were tasting lots of wines not yet ready so he would appreciate a bottle. Christian relented and out came the Dauvissat with an extra glass for me. I now seem to have been adopted into German wine society! Champa meanwhile continued with her squash soup!
A classic debate now began, to what extent was the

Dauvissat Premier Cru not ready, when would it be ready, how did it compare with my 2012 from the previous visit, and …….. how might it compare with a Raveneau from the same year! Good grief, Albert now called Christian back and ordered a 2014 Chablis made by Dauvissat's neighbour, Francois Raveneau so we now have 3 bottles of rock-star status Chablis in front of us from Dauvissat , Raveneau, Fèvre, that might cost £400-500 in a UK restaurant!

My title of this section "In vino veritas et amicitia" translates from the Latin … "In wine there is truth and friendship". The evening I have described continued for some time with Champa eventually adding her own teetotallers views; what more could demonstrate the veracity of that Latin phrase as three Germans, a Frenchman, an Englishman and a Nepalese woman meet as relative strangers, share their evening, and depart as friends with shared contact details for the future. So let me say it again …. "it's not about the wine"!

Beaune
It's an 80 miles journey from Chablis to Beaune and using the A6 it takes less than 90mins, so we were checking into

our hotel by 10.30am. We had chosen the Hotel de La Cloche just outside the ring road, but only a few minutes walk into Place Carnot in the centre of the town, mostly because it had its own car park at the back of the hotel. Our plan was a simple one for today; first, a walk around town and a lunch at Le Grand Cafe de Lyon, calling in at the Nuiton Beaunoy cooperative to buy some wines Sharon had asked me to get for her, then at 4pm going in to Pommard to meet Steve and William at Domaine Michel Rebourgeon for a cellar tasting.

This cellar tasting was our third at "Rebourgeon" and very different this time because it included tasting the wine from this years harvest which was still in the stainless steel tanks. The liquid that was poured into our glasses was a rich frothy purple, youthful and vibrant, obviously cloudy but the freshest, fruitiest and alcoholic grape juice I had ever tasted! Remember that this was less than two months after harvest so there was a lot of technical conversation between Steve and William about specific gravity and alcohol content, pH/acidity, malolactic fermentation and whether more "punching down" of the skin crust on the surface of the liquid in the tank was needed. They seemed to reach some sort of decision as we descended into the cellar with its musty smells and dark walls though I was oblivious to it as I stared in wonder again at the rows of barrels all waiting to empty their contents into the classic shaped bottles of Burgundy.

As in previous years it all became a blur as we tasted barrels of Volnay, Pommard, and basic Bourgogne Pinot Noir, all red and some of premier cru status such as Pommard Les Rugiens, and I'm always very conscious that this is business to Steve and William, it's not just an hours entertainment for me but a privilege to be included as they conduct a serious personal analysis of a product worth millions of Euros. I don't distract them with loads of touristy questions as they interpret signals sent from palate and nose to brain into decisions on whether a particular barrel is ready for bottling; I'm very happy to observe, but next time when I can get them away from the cellar and with a glass of wine in our hands somewhere relaxing I will ask my 101 questions of them both!

And where was my teetotal wife during this hour of alchemy you might ask? Sitting on the cellar steps with infinite patience but ready for an early dinner, which for the record and as a recommendation we had an hour later in Beaune at Bar Le Cercle just a few minutes walk from our hotel towards the town centre.

This is a lovely homely brasserie with a rural-rustic menu serving all the classics such as Coq au Vin, Boeuf Bourguignon, Escargots, Jambon Persille, Steaks, Omelettes ...... and a wine list of local red and white wines at reasonable prices by the glass or bottle. It has a long wooden bar, wooden tables with the ubiquitous red checked tablecloths, and walls decorated with wine related prints and paintings. Service was very friendly, food was excellent with large portions of coq au vin with rice for Champa and boeuf bourguignon with chips for myself. A couple of glasses of Cotes de Beaune were involved too before we returned to our hotel and slept extremely soundly.

The most famous wine chateau in the world!
Across hundreds of years the Clos de Vougeot has developed far beyond its simple beginnings. Wine is no longer made at the Chateau, it is a museum as well as being the headquarters of The Confrérie des Chevaliers du Tastevin. It has had a turbulent history through to its modern day fame and the continuing celebration of good Vin de Bourgogne and friendship in wine around the world.

It was a bitterly cold morning. The hedges were covered with frost as were the vines, at least those we could see that hadn't disappeared into the fog that had enveloped the whole of the Côte d'Or slopes of Burgundy. It was late November so what did we expect?

We parked on the main drive leading up to the chateau, excited to be visiting such a historic place, but shivering with the cold. It was no better inside, what did we expect ..... a 500 year old chateau with central heating? We bought our tickets and began to follow the guide map through the different chambers .... a kitchen, a banqueting hall, cloisters, a tool room, and then a series of rooms containing exactly what we came to see .... huge wine presses, massive barrels, all in oak and hundreds of years old. There's more to this chateau than just empty buildings which sadly is the experience one gets in most French chateaux!

But this really is the most famous chateau AND vineyard in the world, Chateau du Clos de Vougeot, also known as Clos Vougeot. It's a wall-enclosed vineyard, a clos, in the Burgundy wine region of France. An essential pilgrimage for wine lovers if ever there was one. It was created by Cistercian monks of Cîteaux Abbey only a few kilometres away. The land making up the vineyard was purchased by the Cistercians, or donated to them, between the 12th century to the early 14th century and was completed with a wall built around it, by the year 1336. It served as the flagship vineyard of the Cistercians, and has been a highly recognised name for centuries, probably the most famous in the whole world today. I will write much more of this place, along with others, in a later chapter on **Wine with History.**

Eventually the cold overcame us and we left after an hour or so of exploration and drove about a kilometre down the road and into the village of Vougeot itself to visit La Grande Cave de Vougeot.

This is one of those strange places in France that I've often been a little wary of, it's not a vineyard cave, it's not a cooperative either. In one sense it's a shop, but a very select shop that sells only the wines made by contributing winemakers from or around the village. There's one in Pommard too, but this one sells the only wines of the vigneron Charles Vienot, Morin Pere & Fils, Antonin Rodet, Louis Bouillot and Vincent Girardin, with these winemakers producing wines from 80 different appellations in Burgundy's Cote de Nuits. I tasted a dozen or so red wines, all Pinot Noir obviously. Eventually I settled on a Fixin, Clos du Chapitre 2015 made at Domaine Charles Vienot.

"Clos du Chapitre is one of six Premier Cru climats in the commune of Fixin, just south of Dijon in the Burgundy wine region. The vineyard, planted to Pinot Noir, lies on the hillside just to the south of the village of Fixin itself. Its wines, like most of those from Fixin, are weighty and rustic with bright fruit flavors; not as elegant or refined as those from the neighboring commune of Gevrey-Chambertin."

I thought this was the best value for money, a Premier Cru wine that cost €38 per bottle and, at that price it was roughly mid way across the range of wines I tasted. I bought a case and we drove back to Beaune for an evening meal with our friends the Rebourgeon family. Job done!

Dinner with the winemakers

We stood just outside the entrance of our hotel for only a few minutes before we were picked up by the Rebourgeon family, Steve, Delphine, and their son William. They have a second son, Samuel, who is slightly younger than William but who has a different view of his future career other than winemaking. William on the other hand is completely dedicated to the family business and being a winemaker, having been educated at the Beaune college of oenology and also having spent some time working at a vineyard in Australia. Add to that his daily routine work of tending vines, harvesting, fermenting, bottling, marketing, entertaining tourists as well as knowing a heck of a lot of other young winemakers in the area and you have a young rising star of Burgundy!

We drove to the winemaking village of Rully, only about 30mins from Beaune, but done at night time and with a local using known local roads I have no idea how we got there or even where we were until we parked outside the entrance to Hotel Vendangerot in the village centre at Place Saint-Marie.

Rully is one of 5 recognised winemaking villages in the Cotes Chalonnaise along with Bouzeron, Mercurey, Montagny and Givry. Their wines, along with most of this part of Burgundy are 70% white and 30% red with all of the red being Pinot Noir and, maybe surprisingly, NOT all of the white wine being Chardonnay!

I asked William to choose a bottle of wine as an aperitif for while we were perusing the menu and, after he'd had a word with the sommelier, a bottle of wine chilling in a bucket of ice arrived. William inspected the bottle and after taking a quick sniff and slurp said "Bon"! It was a Bouzeron 2016, Domaine de Villaine meaning it was an Aligote, Burgundy's other white wine grape that had all but disappeared in the mad scramble of the 1990s to plant every square metre of land here with Chardonnay. Our conversation naturally then turned to the issue of the resurgence of Aligote based wines here and it seems that a group of young winemakers had begun planting of this grape in the Bouzeron area and had enabled it to be classified as its own recognised appellation in 1998 as opposed to being rated as an inferior wine and labelled "Bourgogne Aligote". William told us that Domaine de Villaine is one of the top vigneron in Bouzeron and that the chief winemaker is Pierre de Benoist, the nephew of the owner Aubert de Villaine. It was a lovely wine, quite acidic and lean wine up front, but if you have the patience to wait a few sessions before passing judgement you will find a longer citrus finish. Just as I remember it from 1987 when I first came across it in Domaine Ropiteau in Meursault, though since that time it had become more familiar as an addition to cassis to make a Kir aperitif in fancy restaurants, but no chance of that here, it was too good for that.

We had a second bottle to go with the meal as we enjoyed each others company, exchanging stories of our families and association with wine …….. collecting it, drinking it, and of course making it. Before we knew it almost 3 hours had passed and it was time to depart. It had been a memorable evening and one we had all wished to repeat, but unfortunately from mid 2019 due to some personal health issues and of course Covid 19 across 2020 it hasn't been possible. We keep in touch via email however knowing that each of us shares a bond of friendship glued together by wine, whether that be a bottle of the humble Aligote from Bouzeron, or a bottle of Premier Cru Les Rugiens from Pommard ….. made by William of course!

Chapter 15
Wine and Celestial Bodies

Terroir and biodynamic are two words that have featured in some of the earlier chapters and I have used them to enhance the descriptions of either tasting experiences or when exploring particular landscapes. I am no expert on either of these topics and what I have learned has come from either some real experts such as Hugh Johnson and Jancis Robinson in their stellar books I shall refer to shortly, from internet articles written by very experienced wine professionals, from vigneron friends in Burgundy, from tastings with winemakers, and lastly from wandering around vineyards in Alsace, Chablis, Pommard, Chinon, Sancerre, and Chateauneuf du Pape. I was never trying to become an expert, or merely trying to understand why wine x tasted different from wine y, it was all about engaging better with the people who made the wine, understanding their enthusiasm and their passion, feeling the effort they and their ancestors had taken to develop the land in which their vines were planted over the centuries in many cases. Read this quote from Alder Yarrow in one of his regular interesting posts on his blog, Vinography. Do you agree with what he says, are you one of those people he is describing?

"When I speak to many wine drinkers, they often express a similar sentiment. They tell me that they really enjoy wine, but they don't know much about it. With varying degrees of embarrassment or chagrin, they describe their interest in experiencing more of what wine has to offer, but then go on to cite any number of factors that they see as barriers to their own ideal relationship with wine. How do we actually progress from habit to true love affair? Most people believe what they are missing involves knowledge that could fill several textbooks. Certainly the difference between a true connoisseur and an enthusiastic wine lover involves quite a bit of understanding of wine's complexities. But some things are more important than book learning."

In his post he goes on to list five essential characteristics of a wine lover that he believes can enhance our relationship with wine, and these are Curiosity, Hedonism, Forgiveness, Patience and Cameraderie, and it is the first one, Curiosity, that has driven me to better understand terroir and biodynamic winemaking. I hope it's driving you too as you read this chapter, and the next few, that emphasise the title of this book It's Not About the Wine! I also hope you'll read that article by Alder Yarrow, it's an inspiration. And .... it will completely change your approach to buying and enjoying wine.

Terroir
In Chapter 6 I described a horizontal tasting I'd had of 4 Cabernet Franc wines in Chinon, all of the same 2011 vintage but each from vines growing in different soils. The

difference was astounding, as was the price range, and the young man helping us provided a real eye opener into the effect of this ONE aspect of terroir which piqued my curiosity beyond belief. After the tasting Champa and I searched our memories for having seen or experienced anything similar, because for years we had focused our interest mostly on grape variety, country and region without much else. What we recalled however was our first visit to Chateauneuf du Pape in the South of France and seeing the vines of Syrah and Grenache baking in the hot sun and sitting in fields of cobblestones! The "galets" are large stones, smoothed and rounded by glacial or water action, which protect the vine roots from the hot sun during the day, then release their heat to keep the roots warm at night. Genius! But this is as much a part of the Rhône terroir as the clay, limestone and schist of the Loire terroir. Different terroir, different grapes, different wine styles. Horses for courses.

The simplest way to think about this is to reflect on any gardening you may have done. Which soils are best for rhododendrons or azaleas? The answer is ericaceous or acid soil. Which soils are best for growing geraniums? The answer is alkaline soil. Which plants need full sun and which plants need shade? I think you're getting the point, the simplest point, so let's take a simplistic view of terroir.

First, there is no simple definition nor an alternative word in the English language; you can read about it all you like, but you won't grasp the concept and it's importance until you speak to a French winemaker, especially in Burgundy. It is terroir that determines where a wine permitted to be labelled as Pommard differs from a wine labelled as Volnay, and where the 7 Grand Cru fields of

Chablis finish and where the Premier Cru fields begin. So, what are these components of terroir that the French, and increasingly the rest of the world especially now in Argentina, California, New Zealand and South Africa are so concerned with? Well, according to The Oxford Companion to Wine (Jancis Robinson) they are:

1. Soil as determined by its geology and pedology as its chemical characteristics
2. Climate as measured by temperature and rainfall.
3. Sunlight Energy received per unit of land surface area.
4. Relief or Topography comprising elevation, slope and aspect.
5. Hydrology or soil-water relationship.

Here's an example of the soil component:

"The Chardonnay vines of Chablis are located in a sedimentary basin. This low-lying zone, once under the ocean, was gradually covered by the material that today make up the soil and subsoil of the Chablis wine region. The vineyards of Chablis have one sole religion!: the Kimmeridgean," writes Jacques Fanet in his book "Les Terroirs du Vin" published by Hachette. The Kimmeridgean is a geological age in the Upper Jurassic epoch, around 150 million years ago. In Chablis, one finds subsoils of gray marl which alternate with bands of limestone, and sometimes very rich in fossils"

So there's the first clue, this region was once under an ocean and the subsoil in Chablis is known as Kimmeridgean, so named after the village of Kimmeridge in Dorset, England. The subsoil is full of Exogyra Virgula, a small, comma-shaped oyster that is characteristic of the marl from the Middle and Upper Kimmeridgean! Now there's a surprise, The Chardonnay grapes of Chablis are growing in and fertilised by oyster shells! It is in this very particular subsoil, which in places breaks the surface, that the wines of Chablis draw their unique character, their purity, their sophistication and minerality. THAT is a striking example of terroir, and part of the reason why it is virtually impossible to replicate a chardonnay based wine that tastes exactly like a Chablis.

It's a similar tale involving my favourite grape, the Pinot Noir, especially if it's from Burgundy. However, I have tasted more BAD Pinot Noir than I care to recall, always semi justified with the statement "it is a very difficult grape to grow and to make wine from!" Now this is undoubtedly true, but it's no excuse for still trying to get top price for a poor wine just because it's made from Pinot Noir.

The problem is that for the last 50 years or so the rest of the world has been trying to emulate the Burgundy wines of Pommard, Volnay, Gevrey Chambertin, all villages making wine from the Pinot Noir grape, and ALL with a specific terroir that even leads to a Pommard being different from a Volnay despite these two villages being next door to each other! But with the notable exception of a few in California the vast majority have come nowhere near to succeeding. Lighter in colour than a Cabernet Sauvignon or a Shiraz it has more subtle aromas and flavours too; strawberry, raspberry, cherry, vanilla, earthy aromas like mushroom or smokey cigar-like. These wines have less tannin to so you get less of the astringent effect on the tip of your tongue in younger wines. They are long-keeping too so definitely worth buying for keeping, not as investments, but in maybe five years time to be drinking a bottle worth £50 that you only paid £15 for!

So, Burgundy Rules OK! as far as Pinot Noir is concerned as the winemakers combine their traditions with modern technology, extracting every ounce of flavour from a grape nurtured in harmony with its terroir. Terroir is everything for this grape including soil, climate, elevation, facing direction and drainage.

Therefore the big problem in finding a red burgundy substitute is caused by how the Pinot Noir grape variety is so terroir "conscious". It is so susceptible to so many detail terroir components: soil type, climate especially mean temperature, length of season and frost risk, aspect ..... eg south facing, slope, altitude, latitude, rainfall. It is no wonder that growing Pinot Noir outside Burgundy is so difficult and that prices are so high. But, for those who love a Californian or New Zealand version, don't misunderstand me, it's all about personal taste and nothing else.

So, in recent months whenever I couldn't see a decent Burgundy on a restaurant or wine bar menu I've turned to .... a Malbec for a red wine and a Sauvignon Blanc for a white. Malbec is grown in the Cahors region in the South West of France with the grape also known as Auxerrois or Cot Noir. Previously it has been blended with two other grapes, Merlot and Tannat to give dark inky black wines loaded with tannin giving it great ageing potential, and recent evidence supports the theory that Cot Noir originated in .... Burgundy! More recently in France winemakers have been developing wines unblended as 100% Malbec with great success.

However it is Argentina that is rightly becoming famed for its Malbec based wines. Historically Argentina depended on Spanish colonisers for their first imports of the vinifera vines which arrived direct from Spain in 1541. Then a year later and also in 1550 seeds and vines were imported from Peru. Then in 1556 more vines arrived from Chile. But these imports were NOT Malbec. However it was in 1851 that the provincial governor, Domingo Faustino Sarmiento received grapevine cuttings from France brought by Miguel Pouget, a French agronomist, and amongst them was Malbec. Despite this, it wasn't until more than 100 years later in the late 20th century that Argentinian winemakers realised that they had underplanted a grape vine that could produce higher quality premium wines, which led to Malbec becoming the most predominant and widely planted grape in the country.

But none of this explains my sudden curiosity in Argentinian Malbec beyond quaffing a cheerful version in a restaurant when a decent Burgundy isn't available. The clues are in my opening paragraphs above, first that the Malbec/Cot/Auxerrois grape originated in Burgundy, and second that about 10 years ago one particular winemaker, Sebastian Zuccardi, began experimenting with growing vines in different parts of his land with differing soils. These soils are diverse, caused by the shifting rock, sand and chalk of the Andes mountains. Today, he has around 20 different wines each year, all Malbec, all because of terroir …….. soil variations especially, but also related to climate and altitude. And so now instead of making only homogenised and blended wines from a single grape into a single wine, Zuccardi and many others are carefully crafting quite different wines with the terroir-driven Malbec grape.

So, there's four examples of terroir and how it affects which grapes grow best in which soil, how even growing the SAME grape in slightly varying terroir can give different flavours, and how winemakers around the world are increasingly exploiting terroir to make wines of individual character, "terroir driven", instead of homogenous blends that always taste the same. But some winemakers are going one step further, a giant step further, and taking a biodynamic approach to wine production.

Biodynamics

Biodynamics in agriculture has been around for a long while, an approach to farming that was begun by Austrian philosopher Rudolf Steiner in the early 1920s, way ahead of the organic farming movement. Steiner was a social reformer who also proposed the use of agricultural practices based on the lunar calendar and astrological influences, hence the chapter title about celestial bodies. So, to put together all aspects of his approach to winemaking, biodynamics is based on a holistic approach which treats the vineyard as a whole system. This includes the vines, the terroir, the winery and its equipment, the winemaker, and any method of pruning, ploughing, fertilising and controlling pests. Also, adding in the celestial bits, various operations are to be carried out based on the phases of the moon. Seriously!

I first came across biodynamics in 2015 in Alsace during a tasting at Domaine Francois Baur in Turckheim. I had already had a tasting at the wine cooperative in the village and during a tasting of the Riesling at Baur I expressed an opinion that this wine seemed more complex, longer finish, more flavour. The lady hosting the tasting then said it was due to their biodynamic methods which she then proceeded to tell me about. Since that time I have had separate discussions about it with Richard Rottiers at Domaine Des Malandes in Chablis where I had seen their vines being weeded and aerated by a white horse pulling a small plough, and at Domaine Michel Rebourgeon in discussions with William, the young winemaker there who is gradually introducing the technique to their various parcels of land.

There are different aspects of biodynamics that have fascinated me, aspects that go beyond the obvious banning of pesticides and insecticides. For example, everything from pruning to harvesting, is controlled by the biodynamic calendar which categorises root days, flower days, fruit days, and leaf days. Fruit days are meant for harvesting, leaf days for watering, root days for pruning and on flower days, the vineyard is left alone. Another interesting aspect is the use of different manure and feed preparations including yarrow, chamomile and nettle and .... a manure compost that has been stuffed into cows horns and buried in the soil to overwinter! No, I am not making this up!

There is a limit to what I can write here, but if your curiosity has been tickled at all I have added a few links for easy to read articles in the Reference section at the end of the book.

Chapter 16
Wine with Philosophy

"A bottle of wine contains more philosophy than all the books in the world"
Louis Pasteur

Since I was a student, over fifty years ago, I have had an enduring interest in wine. Alongside this interest I have also been fascinated by what the great philosophers have to say about how to live a valuable and gratifying life. They are connected. Each was a diversion, a release from the intensity and microscopic detail of researching in chemistry for a PhD back in the '60s when we were young! A small group of us, led by our professor, not only drank wine … we studied it, tasted it like pros, and even made it! At the same time I found it hard to read any books that weren't related to analytical chemistry, detection limits, spectroscopy, voltammetry …… until I discovered the Ancient Greek and Roman philosophers, especially Socrates, Plato, Aristotle and Epicurus.

Wine and Philosophy, completely different topics but somehow they have conflated into one great hydra ……… and even a metaphor (or an antidote) for old age. This is especially significant when combined also with travel and culture and Buddhism, the latter being obvious with my wife from student days being from Nepal.

A few years back we visited the winery of Domaine Pierre & Bertrand Couly in Chinon, France, where they had a gigantic exhibition arranged within the room containing over a dozen stainless steel tanks of wine awaiting bottling. Hanging above each tank was a large coloured photo, a closeup image of a baby, another one of a teenager studying, all the way round to a very old woman with a deeply lined face.

We sat for some time taking in the meaning of this exhibition, with each image also surrounded with words describing a life stage, such as birth, infancy, youth .... old age ...... It was a brilliant collection of images, but also a complete metaphor between life stages and the stages of wine maturation, from bottling, to drinking well, to apogee/peak, to steady decline and finally death. Yet there was something more in this metaphor, an allusion to how one should "be" at each life stage as written by those philosophers from Ancient Greece as well as considering a psychological approach to life as described by Erik Erikson in his Eight Stages of Psychosocial Development.

I shan't burden you here with a discussion of the stages but I will refer to the final stage which Champa and I are well into! This is the stage in which we fall into Despair or Positive Reflection (Ego Integrity) with Despair being for the "forever young brigade". The FYB, as defined by Daniel Klein in his book Travels With Epicurus, is made up of those folks who are into cosmetic surgery, wear clothing too tight or bright, act as if they were teenagers. Each to his own we say, but not for us as we focus on a positive reflection of our lives, together with an existential focus on the here-and-now in a mindful way. And this brings me to wine, wine tasting and Epicurus.

Epicurus was certainly NOT an epicurean in the sense that we use the word today, he was not a seeker of hedonistic pleasure instead having a Zen-like attitude about his senses: for example when eating a simple bowl of lentils, he would take his time to experience all the subtle delights of their flavour, delights that rival those of more extravagantly spiced fare. Two of his quotes:

"It is not what we have, but what we enjoy that constitutes our abundance"
"Before you eat or drink anything, carefully consider with whom you eat or drink rather than what you eat or drink, because eating without a friend is the life of the lion or the wolf."

So, let's combine the philosophy of Epicurus related to "enjoying the wider moment" of a glass of wine with the psychological life stages of Erikson and positive reflection in old age and this brings me to my final pair of philosophers.... Sartre and Husserl and the beginning of existentialism. Consider this quote from At The

Existentialist Cafe by Sarah Bakewell.

"Paris, near the turn of 1933. Three young friends meet over apricot cocktails at the Bec-de-Gaz bar on the rue Montparnasse. They are Jean-Paul Sartre, Simone de Beauvoir and their friend Raymond Aron, who opens their eyes to a radical new way of thinking. Pointing to his drink, he says, "You can make philosophy out of this cocktail!" which led to Sartre's historic quote, "Existence before essence".

So, now to my OWN glass of wine on the table in front of me which "exists" ..... how do I describe it phenomenologically, existentially, and as already said, never mind what is its essence!? Here's what I thought and wrote as I was about to sip from this glass of wine outside a tapas bar in Malaga, Spain:

"The glass is ice cold, frosted even. The first aroma is of honey, almost like an English Mead which is to be expected from a Malaga sweet wine. It's colour is brown, not like an aged red wine, but clear and bright, "sticking" to the sides of the glass which is often referred to as "having legs"! It is very sweet, cloyingly thick with a burnt taste that lingers on the palate and tongue even after swallowing. As a chilled sweet wine it is a perfect match for a warm and sunny afternoon in Spain, sitting

in the middle of the Malaga town centre terrace with my dear wife, looking up at the Moor Alcazar, a historical central feature of the town".

I could have describe my wine in terms of its chemistry and the botany of the vine, adding more about how the wine is made, or the global wine trade or regional classification systems. Maybe I could have added a description of how this bottle was opened and poured, or how about the effects of alcohol on the human body? But none of this would describe this particular wine, my experience of it as an immediate phenomenon, including the environment in which I was drinking it.

Husserl, The German philosopher who established the school of phenomenology, said that, to describe a glass of wine, we should set aside both the abstract suppositions and any intrusive emotional associations, whatever they are! Then we can concentrate on the bright, fragrant, rich phenomenon in front of me now. This setting aside or 'bracketing out' of "add-ons" Husserl called epoché –a term borrowed from the ancient Sceptics, who used it to mean a general suspension of judgement about the world. In other words describe don't judge. He sometimes referred to it as a phenomenological 'reduction' instead: the process of boiling away any extra theorising about what wine 'really' is, so that we are left only with the intense and immediate flavour –the phenomenon. The result, he asserted, was a great liberation. Phenomenology frees me to talk about my experienced wine as a serious topic of investigation.

Now to the crux , the existential question ….. what is wine tasting to me? To begin, it's not about the wine! It's about travel, culture, people, friendship, curiosity, mindfulness….. as well as the more "academic" elements of chemistry, geology, terroir, grapes, process ….. though less so.

We have already described stories from wine travels in France, though we have others from Italy, Spain, USA, Malta ….. in restaurants, wine bars, tabacs, wine cooperatives, domaine winemakers. In all of these places wine is but one part of the whole, a piece of the greater jigsaw of life, a piece that connects to an Epicurean way of life, the final life stage of Erikson focusing on positive reflection, a means of being mindful or existentialist as with Sartre and Husserl.

Tasting wine needs total engagement, not just with the liquid in the glass, but with all the other parts of the jigsaw ….. travel, culture, people, friendship, curiosity, mindfulness. And as Louis Pasteur said:

"A bottle of wine contains more philosophy than all the books in the world", so why not hold this thought as you open your next bottle of wine, are you ready to fully experience it ….. philosophically?

Since that time in Malaga and reading the book At the Existentialist Cafe, philosophy and philosophical musings have been my companion to wine. How could it be otherwise when you visit a wine town like Chinon with streets named after philosophers, the birthplace of Rabelais, and with a brasserie named Cafe Voltaire?

I like many of Voltaire's thoughts and writing, especially about freedom …….. of religion, speech and thought. One of his quotes, "it is dangerous to be right on matters in which the established authorities are wrong" is a personal favourite of mine about the times we are living in. Then there is one of my favourite books that combines wine with philosophy, I Drink Therefore I Am written by England's late great philosopher, Sir Roger Scruton, which I was browsing through one day sitting in the sunshine with my daughter and her husband outside Cafe Voltaire situated in Rue Voltaire in the centre of Chinon.

Generally speaking this is a book about wine, about philosophy, and about the philosophy of wine.

I had reached the final chapter "What to Drink With What", which surprised me by NOT being about matching wine with food, but about matching wine with the writing of some of the great philosophers in history. So for example matching a Vouvray with Plato, a Sauvignon Blanc with Aristotle, and a Chablis with Locke. Scruton's combinations are well thought out and clearly explained as well as being quite humorous. So, what should I do today, should I choose a particular wine to match Voltaire, (Because I am in a wine bar named after him), or should I do it the other way around and seek Scruton's view on the best philosopher to match with a Cabernet Franc, the noble red grape of the Loire Valley in which Chinon is situated and I am ensconced? I chose the latter and as the recommended philosopher up popped ...... Francis Bacon 1561-1626, First Baron Verulam, Lord High Chancellor of England, and the "father of empiricism", I was suddenly reminded of my initial encounter with him. I first read about Francis B 50 years ago when I was doing my PhD in Chemistry (before I studied psychology) and found it fascinating that he was the person who investigated whether keeping a chicken in snow would preserve it in a condition still satisfactory to eat! But, sadly, in doing this experiment in the snow poor old Francis caught pneumonia and died! Now, to finish this bit off I found a quote of his at the time from his essay "The Advancement of Learning" which I wrote as the opening line of my doctoral thesis: *"If a man begins with certainties he shall end with doubts, but if he be content to begin with doubts he shall end with certainties"* which was extremely apt across my three years of research in the field of electrochemistry. But it has stuck with me throughout my whole life, being especially poignant during my psychologist business career as each new corporate project kicked off, reminding me not to make assumptions, to be open minded, and to doubt everything anyone told me until verified. If you're getting confused, let me summarise for you:

1. I'm sitting in a wine bar in Chinon named after one of France's great philosophers, Voltaire.
2. The primary red wine grape of Chinon is the Cabernet Franc.
3. I'm reading a book by Roger Scruton, one of England's greatest philosophers.
4. The book is called I Drink Therefore I Am.
5. In the final chapter of the book, Scruton recommends that one should drink Cabernet Franc while reading or considering the philosophy of Francis Bacon who was a "hero" and conceptual guide of mine during my PhD student days.

So, how about a glass of wine? It has to be a red, from Chinon, a Cabernet Franc as recommended by Scruton. I ask Patrice for a glass from the Domaine Charles Joguet, Charles himself now retired, but a well known artist and philosopher as well as being a well known winemaker. Patrice opens a fresh bottle and pours me a glass, it's a fairly young wine, still a deep purple in colour, quite tannic but with great ageing potential. I glance at the label on the bottle, it's famous, an image of Rabelais, another great French philosopher born locally. Charles Joguet uses the image of Rabelais as his logo. I take in the aroma so distinctive of Cabernet Franc, a first sip, and begin to read Scruton's words about Francis Bacon:

"The author of "The Advancement of Learning" … a worldly politician, brilliant essayist, wide-eyed observer of the human condition, and intellectual iconoclast who single handedly destroyed the grip of Aristotelian science on the Western mind, and taught us how to gain knowledge … [with our eyes and ears]. Any discussion of his insights should proceed by the comparative method. I suggest opening six different bottles of Cabernet Franc, and then pretending to compare and contrast, taking notes in winespeak, while downing the lot! Then one of the company should read Bacon's essay on "Death" after which a long silence would be appropriate".

Now THAT is wine with philosophy!

Let me conclude this chapter by referencing a very interesting article from Neel Burton entitled A Short Philosophy of Wine which set me thinking (in an Epicurean kind of way) more specifically about "what wine has done for me" across my lifetime. As his preface to the more philosophical bits, here's what Neel wrote:

"When you uncork a bottle of mature fine wine, what you are drinking is the product of a particular culture and tradition, a particular soil and exposure, a particular climate, the weather in that year, and the love and labour and life of people who may since have died. If you know how to read it, the wine, like a book, will speak to you of all those things and more."

"Through wine, I have learnt a great deal about geography, geology, agriculture, biology, chemistry, gastronomy, history, languages, literature, psychology, philosophy, religion... By wine, I have communed with, and actually visited, many parts of the world—and should add that wine regions, with their gardened slopes and goldilocks climates, make for the most agreeable destinations. Blind tasting has accelerated my development. It has also taught me about the methods of the mind, and, in the process, made me less bigoted, less dogmatic. On so many levels, wine offers a medium and motivation to apprehend the world. It is, ultimately, a kind of homecoming, a way of feeling at home in the world."

Looking back over our 50 years of messing around with wines I can clearly see how it has played a big part in our lives, as students, as parents, as travellers and now in retirement. Yet one of us is a complete teetotaller, doesn't touch a drop! So, wine is a philosophy in itself! Wine tasting stimulates the senses and provides a window into neuroscience; wine travel broadens the mind into different cultures, geology, geography, history; merely drinking wine is a social activity and one which leads into food and the combining of taste sensations; try learning about these things as you sniff, sip and slurp your way to the bottom of cracked jug in Greece, or as you swirl a Reidal glass of claret in a Michelin restaurant in London, or glug from a flute of champagne in Epernay. It's an existential experience!

Chapter 17
Wine with History

I shall begin this chapter by making the distinction between "history OF wine" and "history WITH wine", with it being the latter that interests me more than the former. Some might think I am splitting hairs or contriving a difference that doesn't exist, but bear with me and form your opinion at the end of the chapter.

History OF wine

A simple example of "history of wine" is provided at L'Imaginarium just outside Nuits St Georges in France, a museum we have visited only once on a very, very hot day when we were seeking somewhere, anywhere to go so as to get out of the heat of a molten summer in Burgundy. It was air conditioned and that was enough for us! Inside it seemed to be organised into 3 areas, a tasting room and shop, an interactive exhibition I really can't remember much about, and finally a very interesting "tour" in which you walked around 3-4 rooms with each containing winemaking tools, implements and equipment from different eras of winemaking. Each room also provided an audio visual show on a big screen which described and walked you around the room before some doors opened automatically to take you into the next room. So, this museum is general rather than specific, broad rather than focused, and on reflection I wasn't convinced I actually learned anything, I have no lasting memories of this place which is nothing more than a contrived building without any history of its own! It has no sense of place, no sense of history.

Another example, but more enjoyable and informative is the Oz Clarke book, The History of Wine in 100 Bottles. I've enjoyed this book and often refer to it one page at a time describing a single issue of Wine History. "Where Did It All Start, 6000 BC" is bottle one, and centres on Georgia as the place where it all began, not Rome, not Greece ..... then there's a page on bottle shapes, one on Appelation Controlee, and another on Extreme Atacama 2010. I thoroughly recommend it .... you're welcome Oz!

Wine WITH history

Now let me change tack, and it might help if you refer back to the chapter on Chablis November, 2018, in which I refer to The Treasure of Vix, probably the largest and oldest wine decanter in the world. Take a look again, is this a description of history of wine or wine with history. Which one is it? Clearly it's the latter, mostly about the history of the Gauls so not about wine history. But, it's the biggest wine decanter in the world and obviously says lots about the Gauls being more civilised than the Romans or modern history give them credit for, so, I categorise this as being wine with history!

There are many perfect examples of wine with history in Burgundy, the most evocative word and place in any wine lovers lexicon. Consider Chateau de Clos de Vougeot, the most revered building to wine officianados and undoubtedly the most famous wine chateau in the world. It doesn't matter whether you like Pinot Noir and Chardonnay or not, nor whether you dislike or can't afford Burgundy wines. This is also the most famous vineyard in the world and one that produces wines sold at staggering prices. It is a wall-enclosed vineyard, a clos in French and an essential pilgrimage for wine lovers if ever there was one. It was created by Cistercian monks of Cîteaux Abbey only a few kilometres away. The land making up the vineyard was purchased by the Cistercians, or donated to them, between the 12th century to the early 14th century and was completed with a wall built around it, by the year 1336. It served as the flagship vineyard of the Cistercians, and has been a highly recognised name for centuries, probably the most famous in the whole world today.

But what many people won't know, and it isn't noted on their website (!) is that the Clos de Vougeot was created by an Englishman, a Saxon, Stephen Harding who was the Abbot of Citeaux for 25 years from the year 1108! The history of Clos de Vougeot is therefore closely connected with that of Citeaux Abbey for the first hundred years or so of its existence, and this needs to be understood before its current "rock star" status can be appreciated. On January 26, 1108, the current abbot, Alberic, died and was soon succeeded by Stephen Harding, the Saxon, and the man responsible for carrying the order into its next important phase. Stephen served Cîteaux Abbey as abbot for twenty-five years and during this time he acquired land for the abbey to develop to ensure its survival and the first of which was Clos Vougeot! In 1133, he resigned as head of the order because of age and infirmity. He died on 28 March 1134 and was buried in the tomb of Alberic, his predecessor, in the cloisters at Cîteaux.

The chateau is currently leased to the Confrérie des Chevaliers du Tastevin. The Fraternity of Knights of the Wine-Tasting Cup is an exclusive bacchanalian fraternity of Burgundy wine enthusiasts. It was founded in 1934 and has chapters worldwide. The primary aims of the organisation are "to hold in high regard and promote Burgundian produce, particularly her great wines and regional cuisine, to maintain and revive the festivities, customs and traditions of Burgundian folklore," and "to encourage people from all over the world to visit Burgundy." Wine with history!

Not too far away from the Chateau de Clos de Vougeot is the Hospice de Beaune located in the centre of the town. Perhaps best known for its annual charity auction which began in 1859 it takes place over the third weekend in November as part of a wider festival of wine in this famous and historic town, the proceeds being used for a modern hospital on the outskirts of Beaune. Irrespective of the festival occurring it's a wonderful place to visit, in fact you are virtually drawn to it, as if by a magnet, as you walk around the centre of Beaune because you keep catching glimpses of the classic Burgundian yellow, orange and brown roof tiles.

It's a small entrance into the "museum" in the Rue de l'Hotel-Dieu which then opens out into a magnificent cobbled courtyard, surrounded by the medieval tiled rooftops all lovingly preserved and cared for. It has to be one of the most awe inspiring views if you have any interest in medieval architecture, and each time I've visited

I stand there for a long time before going inside!

The interior has been well preserved too, remember this was a hospital NOT a winery although there are some strong connections. A ward with a long row of beds each shrouded with red curtains like 4-posters, an apothecaries room, kitchens, a chapel ……. All rooms you would expect to find in a hospice for the poor in the 1400s.

The hospice was founded in 1443 by the Chancellor of France, Nicolas Rolin who decided to help the poor recover from the unrest and plague of the 100 years war. He had researched such hospices in Flanders and Paris and not only created a building, he ensured its continuity by installing a system of management with endowments of vineyards and farms before placing it under the authority of the Pope.

"Today the Hospice wine estate comprises 60 hectares, of which 50 are devoted to Pinot Noir and the rest to Chardonnay. Entrusted to 22 winemakers handpicked by its manager, this exceptional vineyard accounts for 85% of premiers crus and grands crus sold at the November auction, today organised by Christie's auction house, and is the most famous wine charity auction in the world. The proceeds of the sale are used to improve the Beaune hospital's equipment and in the conservation of the Hôtel Dieu itself."

We have many other personal examples of wine with history, especially from our travels around Europe. We have taken several Mediterranean cruises in recent years visiting ports and inland towns along the coasts of Portugal, Spain, France, Italy, as well as the islands of Madeira, Malta, Sicily and Sardinia. In all of these places one "meets" Aristotle, Archimedes, Pliny the Elder,

Hannibal and …….. The Duke of Clarence! Each piece of history was somehow combined with wine, either through drinking something local while gazing at a statue where the person was born or lived, or better still there being a direct comparison pointed out by a tour guide or a wine tasting host. For example, our cruise ship had stopped at Naples for a day and so we visited Pompeii and Herculaneum, both cities being ruined by the eruption of Vesuvius in AD79. At Herculaneum, Luca, our guide was pointing out the rows of amphora near to some amphora shaped holes in what looked like a tiled stone long table or bar.

He explained that these holes contained either snack food such as olives, or the local wine. In essence it could have been a wine bar and he embellished the description by talking about Pliny The Elder and his mistress Rectina and how they could have stood at this same "wine bar" centuries ago. Sadly old Pliny was killed in the firestorm offshore in his ship trying to land and rescue Rectina!

On a different occasion our cruise ship stopped at Funchal, Madeira, for a day. Now, you just cannot stop here and fail to have a tasting of Madeira wine, not to everyones taste, and I'm willing to bet that very few folks reading this have ever tasted it, never mind heard of it!

"To understand why the wine of a little island off the coast of Africa should become world famous, you need to look at an old map. Preferably one from the age of sail" (Oz Clarke, *The History of Wine in 100 Bottles*)

In the 1600s you couldn't just sail from England to America in a straight line, the prevailing winds taking you to Madeira before a new wind could take you across the Atlantic. So, Madeira became an important place of trade, especially for sugar. Ships would also stock up with water and other supplies here, including wine, which the ship captains would adulterate with Brandy to help it survive the voyage. Eventually they began to notice that the adulterated wine underwent a remarkable change, becoming darker and with less acidity. "Eureka" they must have said as they recognised its potential and sold it for multiple times the value of "ordinary" Madeira. Today, there are four styles of Madeira each named after the relevant grape variety; Sercial, Verdhelo, Bual, and Malmsey with the sequence being from light to VERY thick and heavy as I've listed them. So there's a bit of wine with history for a start, but what about The Duke of Clarence?

We walked off the ship and through the port into the town centre, heading for Blandy's Wine Lodge, the main producer on the island established in 1811. Here we sat in a beautiful tasting room, stone floor, dark oak wood walls, door and roof beams, and half-barrels as tasting tables.

We ordered a flight of the main four styles and worked our way through them from the Sercial to the thick syrupy cloying Malmsey. And, did you know that Blandy's make a branded version of madeira called …… The Duke of Clarence. They have others honouring various Dukes of England, but Clarence? Well in Shakespeare's Richard III, his brother George, Duke of Clarence, was accused by Richard and his older brother Edward IV of treason. Deciding he was guilty they drowned him …… in a barrel of Malmsey wine from Madeira. So there you go, more wine WITH history. Hope you agree?

Chapter 18
Wine with Art

Let's begin this chapter with a test! Read the two tasting notes below and then take a look at the two images following. Can you match the words to the images?

1. *"Tropical, lively and clean. Translucent straw yellow colour, intense, fresh aromas of tropical fruit such as banana, passion fruit and mango with hints of lemon and fresh flowers, light and fresh on the palate with high acidity and a clean finish with reoccurring notes of banana and passion fruit."*

2. *"Elegant and feminine with delicate charm. Translucent straw yellow colour, ample yet refined aromas of wild rose, fresh flower petals, white peach, and lime with hints of tropical fruit and white pepper, on the palate soft and mineral, luxurious and well balanced with a fresh almond finish."*

249

Did you match each image to its own tasting notes? The words and images are from Danell Nelson, a Sommelier from Italy, a good friend, and a blogger at www.vinthropology.wordpress.com. In these images from two of her blog posts Danell has encapsulated the aesthetic quality of wine and its link with art and artistic impression through her use of language such as *elegance, balanced, refined, delicate charm* as well as the images themselves …….. In your own opinion, was it the words of Danell's tasting notes or the respective images that stimulated your taste buds, made you imagine the aroma of each wine and how that first sip would taste? Personally, I am more in tune with the visual representation of taste in Danell's artwork for each wine. I can immediately SEE the difference in aroma and taste in each wine, and it makes me wonder if this connected to the psychological process known as Neuro Linguistic Programming in which it is claimed that there is a connection between neurology, language and behaviour. The founders of NLP assert that there are three "states" of mental programming with ONE predominant in each of us, and these are Visual, Auditory and Kinaesthetic. Some people respond best to words and sounds, others to emotions and feelings. In my case I am a "rampant visual" which possibly explains why in much of my life and profession I have communicated best through diagrams of strategies, processes, plans etc. Therefore I could immediately "see" the flavours Danell is highlighting in those two images. More from Danell shortly and the relationship between wine and art.

Brasserie Art
I'm unsure when I first started to notice artwork in

brasseries and wine bars and to make connections between the wine I was drinking, with the place and various pieces of artwork on the walls. I freely admit to being a bit of a philistine regarding art appreciation, although I had started to visit art galleries and museums more often from about 8 years ago. I particularly remember visiting the Museo Ralli to view its collection of contemporary Latin American and European art, with Champa and I spending a couple of hours really fascinated with the exhibits. This propelled us into visiting galleries and specific exhibitions in Denver, New York, Madrid, Paris, Bruges, Kathmandu and others as we travelled the world. So, we became more observant and aware of wine related paintings and prints on brasserie walls in Beaune, Budapest, Prague, Paris, many of which were of the Art Nouveau style we became familiar with having visited the Alphonse Mucha museum in Prague. Try googling "art nouveau champagne posters" as well as "Alphonse Mucha champagne posters" and you'll see what I mean. Recently the same style of art has been used in creating marketing posters of La Chablisienne the wine cooperative in Chablis which seem to portray the essence of their wines as elegant, subtle, captivating, glamorous....... and feminine. I have also seen paintings of Bacchus or Dionysus in wine bars too unsurprisingly, usually versions of those by Caravaggio which, to my mind anyway, give a sense of opulence, wealth, power such as you would expect from a god of wine as well as festivity and theatre. Often the artwork in brasseries has no high value, financially, but it does give the right "atmospherics" to a place and in my opinion adds to the aesthetic quality of the immediate experience.

Wine not the focal point

One of Danell Nelson's blog articles, Painting Pleasure, Drinking Design, goes much deeper into Wine with Art and examines the relationship   and connection between them as she uses *Renoir's Luncheon of the Boating Party* as her subject and vehicle for analysis.

Here's a quote from her article which was also published at Club del Vino.
(https://www.club-del-vino.com/it/painting-pleasure-drinking-design/)

"Renoir's Luncheon of the Boating Party (Le Déjeuner des Canotiers) affords one the rare pleasure of looking in on the cheerful charm of a group of Parisians enjoying a moment of leisure along the Seine river in the late 1800's. Such moments of pleasure and conviviality are often accompanied by wine, as is this case here. In the center of the painting we can see bottles and glasses of wine on the table, around which unfolds conversations, flirtations, sentiments and intrigues. However, as is often case, while wine may be the center piece of such occasions, it is not the focal point but rather the axis on which the wheel turns."

In a subsequent conversation and correspondence with Danell she elaborated on her view of the connection between art and wine, emphasising the obvious sensory nature of each, sometimes occurring in a fleeting moment, but often transporting us to another place such as the painting subject or the origin of the wine. Here's what she said.

"The connection between art and wine through this painting is two-fold. In line with the impressionist style and philosophy, the painting is not a mere representation of a scene, it is an interpretation of all the sensations involved in that fleeting moment. The vivid colours and open brushstrokes allow one to hear the wind rustling through the glass, the river flowing, the glasses clinking, and the voices chattering. One can almost feel the warmth of the sunlight filtering in through the balcony and the intimate crowdedness of the figures leaning in and around each other. It is as if we are really there. Similarly, the true expression of wine lies in its myriad of sensations which transport us, maybe to the place of its origin, but most certainly deeper within the present fleeting moment we are experiencing. This is all without mentioning the playfulness, pensiveness, and conversations so often occasioned by the act of drinking wine as this painting so charmingly captures."

So now we have two connections between Wine with Art, one a use of descriptive images rather than words to denote aromas and flavours, and another whereby the sensory nature of viewing a piece of art is compared to the sensory nature of tasting a wine.

Sculpture in the vineyard

Now let's take a completely different art form that is becoming more connected with wine. Sculpture In The Vineyard is an event that has been held twice, 2015 and 2018, at Bothy Vineyard in Oxfordshire, England, only a 30min drive from our Cotswolds home. When we visited in 2018 there were 300 sculptures exhibited around and between the vines, mostly from 50+ local artists working with wood, metal, stone, and various synthetic materials. The subjects were not wine related but whether it was a bird, a person, an artefact or something completely abstract, you were always aware of being in a vineyard.

We arrived at lunchtime on a Saturday afternoon and even had to queue to park the car it was so busy at this small but perfectly formed vineyard. Here they grow red and white grape varieties with their main focus on a still white Bacchus and a sparkling rose and there was a crowd of people busy at the outdoor tasting area next to various food stalls and a folk group playing English folk music. We were given a catalogue itemising all of the exhibits, each numbered and with its name, artist and price and then set off wandering through the vines. Within 5 min we were nowhere in sight of each other having wandered off in our own directions attracted towards sculptures that caught our eye, either part way down a row of vines or peeping above them. The first one that I walked up to was alongside a long row of Rondo vines, it was gleaming white, made from something synthetic and called Fork in Pollen! As a literal description it was a very large fork, about 5 metres high, sticking into a large spiky ball representing a pollen molecule. Metaphorically, as a pollen allergy sufferer I could completely identify with what the artist was getting at, and to understand this you need to say aloud the sculpture title quickly and rolled together .... forkinpollen! It's something I mutter daily every Spring when tree pollen abounds.

Let's face it, you can take a cynical view of such an event and say that the only reason for it is to market the vineyard and increase wine sales, but I would argue that it's much more than that. Sure, it attracts customers on the day, new and old, but even at a commercial level the objective is to HOLD new customers, and get repeat business from a wider variety of wines on sale. I believe that this can only be achieved however by new customers getting a greater appreciation of wine, it's dependence on the terroir and how the winemaker cares for that terroir as well as the overall landscape. A sculpture exhibition amongst the vines undoubtedly brings in hundreds of people on the day and many of them will start to increase their understanding of the artistry of winemaking as they see the artistry of the sculptor exhibited in this way. I have read of similar exhibitions in Napa, Sonoma, British Columbia and increasingly across Australia which tells me that there is a global movement taking place connecting wine with art that will increase the confidence of people to visit vineyards, try new wines and new grapes, and to engage in conversation about wine. A good thing too!

Salvador Dalí and wine

Did you know that Salvador Dalí was not only a great artist he was a connoisseur of wine too. He categorised the wines he drank into groupings associated with his emotions and his painting; In his book The Wines of Gala, two of my favourite chapters are "Wines of Joy!" and "Wines of Purple!".

The <u>Wines of Joy</u> are simply listed as Beaujolais, Chinon, Bourgueil, Cotes du Rhone, Chianti, Valpolicella, Merlot of Ticino, Rioja, Muscadet, Swiss white wines, Portuguese Vinhos Verdes.

"The Wines of Joy are linked together in a dance, they are

wines to be drunk young, generally in the year following their birth. They mostly give us aromas, perfumes linked to the grape's properties. Beaujolais tops the list offering an array of perfumes from the vegetable world, fruits and flowers too. Peaches, strawberries, apricots cherries, faded roses, iris, violets, all reaching our palate through the retro-nasal passages. Together with taste they compose a symphony of freshness and suppleness so typical of young wines." (The Wines of Gala)

The cells in our sense organs become "excited" when we drink wine, and with these wines specifically the sensations lead to a perception of youth, freshness, newness and "joy" ..... to use this sensation in a metaphorical sense. I get this sensation personally when I drink Beaujolais, usually chilled on a warm summer's day sitting in the garden admiring the colours of the sparkling mesembryanthemum flowers in the sunlight. Typically the Brouilly appellation from Richard Rottiers being my favourite. Then there is the white Picpoul de Pinet, a wine I have added to Dalí's list, a crisp citrussy slightly acidic wine just made to be well chilled with a plate of seafood. My favourite being from Domaine Felines Jourdan. So here's a question: If we want to feel joyful or to be cheered up do we open a bottle of any of these wines and ..... are transformed? Or, is it the other way around such that if we are already feeling joyful should we open one of these bottles to reinforce our existing mood?

The Wines of Purple are listed as Red Burgundy (Pinot Noir), Chateauneuf du Pape (Mostly Grenache), Red Cotes de Provence, Hermitage (Mostly Syrah), Bandol (Mourvèdre and Grenache), Cote Rotie (Mostly Syrah), Madiran (Tannat), Central European Wines, California Wines, Chilean Wines, Argentinian Wines, Swiss Merlot,

South African Wines.

"From the very earliest times, man, whenever he wanted a symbol of wealth, power or dignity has chosen two key colours ….. gold and purple. Royal purple, cardinal purple, Imperial Roman Purple, papal purple. The Greeks in their ceremonies made an extensive use of Tyrenian Purple." (The Wines of Gala)

These wines are heavyweights in the world of wine, full of body and flavour, often with a complexity resulting from a grape blend from a specific terroir and mostly growing in long hours of sunshine. They are prestigious wines too and can be associated with prestigious historical figure such as Roman emperors, Popes, and Dukes of Burgundy with "purple"

My two favourite wines from this list are from the Pinot Noir grape and the Tannat grape. One is a Pommard/ Burgundy, the other is a Madiran (From the South of France). Both quite different in nature but both definitely Purple. For the Pinot Noir I favour the Pommard 1er Cru from Les Rugiens in Burgundy, and for the Tannat a Madiran from Des Tuguets in Gascogne.

(The book is Salvador Dalí's eccentric guide to wine grapes and their origin and is filled with over 140 artworks and collages collected and created by Dalí himself. In keeping with Dalí's efforts to create artwork based on his emotions, memories, and dreams, the artist chose to organize the wines in the book by how they influenced his mood. The groupings are appropriately imaginative classifications including such section titles as "Wines of Frivolity," "Wines of the Impossible," and "Wines of Light." One section in the book also outlines Dalí's method of ordering wine by emotional experience, quoting the artist's famous credo: *"A real connoisseur does not drink wine but tastes of its secrets."*)

2D or 3D?

"The great advantage of a painting is that its expression is contained within the frame of a simultaneous whole. When the viewer lays eyes on a painting, they are met with the entire composition of a moment both captured and interpreted by the artist. Thus, with all visual elements presented at once, it falls on the viewer to do the internal work of perceiving. But even as internal as this process may be, it is nonetheless constituted by a constant negotiation with the external, through the painting itself as well as the signs and symbols extracted from the world by the mind. It is in this tension between internal thought and external material, caught within the prospect of simultaneity, where the cubist work thrives."

In her two blog articles Danell Nelson compares the similarities between what cubism did for how we <u>see</u> things with what Virginia Woolf did for how we <u>read</u> things. Visual art compared with language. Both transform HOW we perceive things with cubism achieving this through a 3D effect and, as Picasso said, *"I paint objects as I think them not as I see them"*. So how does this connect Wine with Art? Well, the effect of any image is relatively instant and holistic, whereas with a paragraph of words we may take a while to read it all before getting "the whole picture"! If we apply this to say, tasting notes, as in my example at the beginning of this chapter, you will "see" what I mean. The internal mind perceives the external image and forms a view, opinions, and judgements of the wine, even up to the point of whether we are likely to love or hate the wine, not the artwork, but the actual wine itself and this is brilliantly and simply highlighted in this quote from a Buddhist Zen master:

"If ten people look at a cloud, there will be ten different perceptions of it. Whether it is perceived as a dog, a hammer, or a coat depends on our mind —our sadness, our memories, our anger. Our perceptions carry with them all the errors of subjectivity." Thich Nhat Hahn

Now, although I broadly understand the concept of cubism and how artists highlight a painting as fragmented objects shown from multiple perspectives .... I am struggling! Nothing wrong with that, I have been a "learning machine" for my entire life and this is a challenge that won't be solved while I'm writing this book. The cubist painting is forcing me to fill in the gaps, to perceive the whole from the fragments which are normally "seen" and represented two dimensionally as in classical paintings. So lets do an experiment with one of Danell's cubist wine paintings and tasting notes and compare it with any of the above two chardonnay paintings and notes:

"Ruby red: a royal colour, a cardinal gem. Saturated, concentrated, glimmering colour; so many of them likened to gemstones: sapphire, garnet, emerald, and turquoise. Colour, cut, clarity and caret. Cranberries, cherries, raspberries, and juniper berries from these small, concentrated clusters of grapes- little fruit, big flavour. Big, black, spicy pepper. Here, in the delta, the Native Americans peacefully picking berries when the Spanish came with their big boats and jewel crested armour and velvet cloaks. Explorers and missionaries and colonists, and then the Gold Rush, and then the Stockton Ship Channel, and then agriculture, and then irrigation, and then houseboats and water sports. Maybe these old vines could tell the story, twisted and gnarly. Saturated in colour, saturated in flavour: zippy, shimmering, glistening acidity; plush, velvet, tannins- balance. Balsamic berry blast to finish, a crimson crush. Colour, cut, clarity and caret."

Now look back at one of the other Chardonnay images. Which one gives you the instant holistic sense of the wine, its aromas and flavours. Is it the classical or the cubist? For me, its the classical 2D painting, but maybe that's a reflection again of differences between individuals in the wiring of our brains, and even how and whether we can smell or taste gooseberry, strawberry, lime, mushroom .... I'll keep trying, and remembering this: *"We cannot explain an orange to someone who has never tasted one. No matter how well we describe it, we cannot give someone else the direct experience. He has to taste it for himself.* Thich Nhat Hahn

Reflections in a label
My final example of wine with art is that winemakers

have increasingly used artwork on their labels, a phenomenon that goes way beyond the labels on bottles from my student days 50 years ago. I have many examples of labels merely showing the name of the wine, the grape, the country, the vintage, and that was it …….. apart from the classic claret labels that would often have an image of the chateau. Nowadays there is artwork everywhere drawing your eye to a specific bottle on a supermarket shelf, a marketing tactic that surely works for the newcomer to wine, because a label showing strawberries and cream or blackberries and apples is going to impart more about the likely wine characteristics than having to turn the bottle round and read the words on the rear label, whether its in a foreign language or not. In the past few years as part of my Wines 101 quest I have bought wines from all over the world, many with alluring artistic labels, which often tells you a lot about the winemaker and the terroir as well as the wine itself. Here's a few I've encountered:

The final travel?

Writing this sequence of chapters on philosophy, history, art and terroir brings me to the final travel chapter of this memoir describing a trip that took place during late 2019. At the time I wondered whether it might be my last such holiday with my family as I was facing a serious operation a month later, but I tried really hard not to let that affect me or them. I was also determined that the week would not just be day after day of wine tastings and visits to vineyards, there was lots of history and philosophy to in and around Chinon to go WITH the wine. And so it turned out as we "encountered" Rabelais, Voltaire, the Plantagenets again, with our Cabernet Franc and Chenin Blanc. England won the cricket World Cup too which we watched on TV near the end of our week, but I didn't think a chapter on Wine with Cricket would be appropriate! But a year has gone by and there has been no wine travel due to the Covid pandemic since that trip to Chinon in 2019, so as you turn the page and read about it I hope that the title of this book, It's Not About The Wine, shines through.

Chapter 19
2019, Loire, Chinon

It was during this holiday in July 2019 that I began to think seriously about writing this book, not to try and earn lots of money from it but to leave some sort of legacy of a hobby that has been with me for 50 years, something that might inspire others to "go beyond the mere alcoholic content and effect of what is in that wine they are drinking". My own interest in connecting wine with history, philosophy, art, and science had been with me for almost 30 years, but it intensified on this trip as I engaged in a much wider and deeper reflection of my whole life. It would be easy to assume that this was because I was a couple of months away from surgery to remove my cancer infected prostate, but that would be 90% incorrect, because the primary cause had originated in a guest article I had written a while back on the blog, Vinthropology, before prostate cancer had been diagnosed. The article was titled "Wine as a Metaphor for Old Age" and used the book Travels With Epicurus by Daniel Klein, and the psychological process and structure The Eight Stages of Man by Erik Erikson as inspiration and background. Each of these two sources led me deeper into philosophy, especially existentialism with Sartre and Husserl as well as Epicurus of course. In this chapter I will not burden you with too much on such philosophy, that will be expanded on much more in my chapter Wine With Philosophy, but there will be hints of it so that you are helped to understand why this holiday of 2019 seems different.

Our journey to Chinon was slower this time, spread over three days. We decided to spend a day in Kent visiting Dungeness, the shingle beach on the coast having once being designated as a desert because of its low rainfall! We spent the night at the Best Western Clifton Hotel in Folkestone, convenient for an early morning start through Eurotunnel and out into France. Next we travelled to Alencon, a half-way point on our drive to Chinon. It was a charming town with lots of restaurants in the centre to choose from, but unfortunately we had chosen one of those box-room inns on the edge of the motorway for convenience, it was clean but with small and tired rooms. We left early the next morning and had breakfast at a motorway service area! We arrived in Chinon after a couple of hours and in time for lunch, parked in the Place Jeanne d'Arc and checked in at our regular hotel, Le Plantagenet, discovering that they had upgraded us to a suite for the duration of our visit. We had a second room booked for our daughter and husband arriving later today and they had been placed in the room next to us, both rooms on the ground floor and opening onto the hotel gardens.

The next day the four of us visited two domaines, both making wine from Chenin Blanc, the predominant white grape around here. In the morning we visited Domaine du

Closel in Savennières and then after lunch a visit to Domaine Pierre & Bertrand Couly on the outskirts of Chinon. I described this day in the opening chapter, It's Not About The Wine, so wont repeat it here but you might want to skip back to reread it because it will give you a flavour of and set the scene for this visit to Chinon.

It's fizz Jim, but not as we know it!

It had been 20 years since Sharon had visited this area of the Loire, and if you asked here to list her top 3 memories from her first trip even 30 years earlier she would say Eurocamp, Moules Mariniere, and .... Gratien & Meyer, one of the top producers of Cremant de Loire in the whole region. So, we drove to Saumur where their massive winery is situated high on the slopes above the River Loire on the outskirts of the town on the D947, but didn't stop yet as it was time for lunch at one of our favourite brasseries in the town centre. We parked as usual at Parking Moliere, also free as usual between 12.00 and 15.00, and walked the short distance to Brasserie de La Bourse. I hesitate to call this a fast food joint because the food is classic French brasserie such as steak-frites, pizzas, and moules marinieres of course, but the service is really fast as the waiters and waitresses almost sprint around the outdoor tables under large umbrellas on the very wide pavement. The road here is closed to traffic, at least at lunchtime anyway.

After lunch we drove back out to Gratien & Meyer and drove to the main building at the top of the hill. Inside is a brightly furnished tasting room with sunlight streaming in through the glass windows that run the length of the room opposite the long bar. We were served by Nils who is from

Sweden, and who took us through their range of Cremant de Loire fizzy wines that really do rival Prosecco and will give many a champagne a run for their money! We had two wines on our list to seek out, first their Cardinal Mousseux Demi Sec, a red sparkler made from Cabernet Franc and second a white Cuvee Flamme Brut which most importantly I had spotted in Wines 1001 Book and added to my bucket list. As described in the book:

"Cuvee Flamme has a vital pale gold colour, while the cordon of the mousse is steady, regular and elegant. The wines aromas are both profound and pretty, the dominant scents being those of springtime woodland flowers. Outside champagne, Flamme is one of the very few sparkling wines to come anywhere near to the taste of champagne, with its delicate, mineral fruitiness combined with a depth of complex mature flavours."

Since being founded in 1846 there's been a long history of politics, quarrying, war, and shrewd business development here as well as the winemaking itself. The company own a champagne "house" too and I will add more in my chapter on Wine With History. There's a short but interesting tour and exhibition behind the tasting room that will give you an introduction to the 150 years journey of the company which we had viewed before so didn't take today. We left with cases of the two wines we had come to taste at €7.46 for the Cardinal Mousseux and €10.35 for the Cuvee Flamme.

A walk back in time
Although this holiday was a family affair with our daughter and her husband joining us, and being a great

occasion to visit vineyards, chateau, museums and outstanding restaurants together .... plus a few iconic wine bars of course, each morning we would all do something different for morning exercise pre breakfast, cycling, tai chi, or walking. My walks took me around vineyards, the castle walls and the deserted narrow streets of old Chinon with only my iPhone in my pocket, often seeing buildings, signs, street names, statues and chapels that go unnoticed during a busy afternoon with the streets full of wandering tourists or busy locals. There is an eerie but welcome silence at this time of the morning as well as cool air that within a few hours would be 15 degrees higher.

Most mornings I would leave the hotel around 6.45am after my ritual morning cup of tea made with leaf from the Dhankuta estate in Nepal, so yes, I'm a bit of a tea geek too! Typically I would take the lift up to the Chateau area from the car park, Parking de la Breche, behind and through the arch at the end of the Place du General de Gaulle, and this meant that most of my walk would be downhill or flat and I could concentrate on my surroundings and their connections with history, people, culture, and philosophy even.

The proper name of the chateau here is Forteresse

Royale de Chinon, a bit of a giveaway really because of its connections with royalty and that what you see is a fortress rather than a palace. You can best understand this looking up from the opposite bank of the River Vienne in the Le Faubourg Saint-Jacques area of Chinon where the defensive nature of the fortress is obviously created by the river, steep hillside, towers and surrounding walls. Historically the fortress, and therefore the town , connects with Henry II of England and his wife Eleanor of Aquitaine, their son Richard The Lionheart and King John , with the first three buried at Fontevraud Abbey a few miles away. It also served as a prison in 1307 when the Knights Templar were arrested with their leader, Jacques de Molay, held here before his trial and execution.

Then, Charles VII installed his court here in 1425 during the Hundred Years War with Joan of Arc visiting in 1429 to pledge her allegiance to him. But in 1631 the fortress was no longer a royal fortress and fell into the ownership of the Duke of Richelieu who held little interest in it. In the mid 1800s many of the fortifications were removed opening up the banks of the Vienne for trade and traffic.

The views from the chateau show the compact nature of the medieval town below and a sweeping vista across the river and the plains beyond. Exiting the adjacent grounds of the fortress reminds me immediately that this is a "cultural" wine town because opposite is the monopole vineyard Clos de L'Echo once owned by the Rabelais family, and to my right is the Caves de Silene of Charles Joguet whose domaine logo is the head of Francois Rabelais the French Renaissance philosopher, writer and humanist. It's downhill from here and there's a gravelled footpath that descends alongside the fortress walls and slightly above the Avenue Francois Mitterand, curving around to the Caves Plouzeau wine shop and the Quai Pasteur.

From here I would now enter the narrow Rue Haute Saint-Maurice, a long straight lane with no room for two cars to pass, but completely deserted at this time of day. You cannot help yourself stopping every few yards along here to inspect the half timbered medieval buildings so well preserved and cared for. Some are dwellings, others are obviously commercial with the complete mix of restaurants, hotels, gites, shops selling books, antiques, paintings, wool, and the occasional boulangerie or patisserie. Despite the modernity of use, you can definitely feel the age and history of the environment.

Eventually the Rue becomes the Rue Voltaire with the compact and friendly wine bar, Cave Voltaire, run by Patrice, and then the brasserie A la Pause Rabelaisienne at the end. The names of these philosophers and humanists are repeated and honoured for their contribution to French culture in this town and you will also find Rue Diderot and Rue Jean Jacques Rousseau depending on which route you take back to the Hotel Plantagenet. Choose a different route and you will find a large statue of Rabelais by the river or metal motifs of his head on the side of buildings. Either way this is a refreshing and enlightening start to the day as return to Place Jeanne d'Arc with her statue in the centre, especially now to be followed by a cracking breakfast at the hotel.

Down on the farm

"Monk, doctor, writer, botanist, and translator, Rabelais was one of the most enlightened minds of the Renaissance. Behind the comic, laughter-inducing exterior of his work lie some very important issues; war, education, religion, marriage, and the question of the Other. He was a humanist, his writing full of the new ideas both he and Erasmus held dear."

The Musee Rabelais is situated in the tiny hamlet of La

Deviniere, just 4 miles outside Chinon. It was the last day of our July holiday and we had saved our visit so that we wouldn't (as usual!) just be focusing on getting home! It was only 10.15am as we parked and stepped out into the searing heat already 30 degrees. Walking up a slight incline through the vines towards the farm where Rabelais was born, we could see the Chateau Coudray Montpensier, a place not open to the public but we had once visited by accident and were permitted to explore the grounds. It features in the Rabelais novels as does most of the landscape around here, nowadays "painted" with vines, wheat and sunflowers across rolling hills as far as you can see.

Francois Rabelais was born in 1494 and died in 1553, he was the son of Antoine, a rich landowner and lawyer. He spent all of his childhood years at this farm, now a simple but interesting museum which outlines his life and works, most notably his literary work especially the novels Pantagruel and Gargantua. Both are rich in comedy and satire with the royal court and the clergy often the target. They were originally written for a learned audience, but the English translation is very easy to read. Initially he studied law, then became a novice monk, then studied medicine at the University of Montpellier, so his literary work came later and frequently opened him to persecution and prosecution because of his bawdy humour style of lampooning authority figures. But …… he had powerful friends and protectors who must have silently agreed with his satirisation of Charles V (The Holy Roman Emperor), pedagogy, the medical profession and religious doctrine.

It only took around an hour to explore the museum which includes a barn, a dovecote, extensive cellars, living quarters and gardens. The rooms are not furnished as they would have been at the time of Rabelais living here, but rather are filled with displays relating to his complete life such as paintings and sculptures of him, documents, books and manuscripts. The cellars were really quite interesting as well as being extensive, apparently being used for livestock but I'm none the wiser as to why this was. Although it didn't take long, it was a very atmospheric visit, having read his novels and researched his life a little it was as though I could feel his presence, but maybe that's because several parts of this landscape are described in those novels.

I've written above about recognising French culture and how it is embedded in their towns, streets, bars, statues, and CHINON is the place to recognise it. A statue of Rabelais along the river and at the entrance to the Place General de Gaulle, a street named after him, a wine bar bearing his name, his family vineyard, Clos de L'Echo, run by Domaine Couly Dutheil still going strong, and ..... probably the best red Cabernet Franc based Chinon wine made by Charles Joguet with a famous image of Rabelais on every label. I think he would have approved!

Homeward bound

And so we travelled home after another family holiday in a French wine town, but with wine playing a secondary role in our activities. Sharon and Michael drove back to England via Calais and Eurotunnel, while Champa and I journeyed up to Caen and onto Brittany Ferries for a relaxing 6 hours voyage across the English Channel to Portsmouth. It had been a thoughtful few days with more time spent "engaging" with history and philosophy than on wine tasting and I was thinking about this watching the numerous commercial tankers sailing through the channel rather than across it as we were. I'd also spent quite some time in Chinon lazing around the place just sitting in wine bars and brasseries trying to piece together why we kept coming here, why we usually stayed in the same hotels, why we visited the same vigneron for wine tasting and buying. And slowly but surely I began to realise the reasons were related to people, history, culture, and friendships. It wasn't about the wine at all!

Chapter 20
England!

In our student days English wine had the taste of blackberries, blackcurrants, gooseberries, dandelion .... and that's because it was made from them! I made them too, but did once make a wine from a tin of grape juice which won a prize at our Glasgow wine club! Then a few small vineyards "appeared" in England and were explored by the curious, ignored by the serious and ridiculed by the supercilious. But not any more, despite the EU trying hard:

"When it comes to local wine, however, the regime of insane regulations begins to bite. An enterprising neighbour planted vines at nearby Noah's Ark, where he made a crisp dry white from Riesling, Scheurebe and similar varietals. He worked seriously and scientifically and named his product 'Cloud Nine', in honour of the crows, ninth pair of creatures to enter Noah's Ark, who chattered contentedly in the clouds around the mast. And he proudly put his product on sale as 'English Table Wine'. A European Directive told him to pour the stuff down the drain or risk prosecution. The offending word was not 'table' or 'wine' but 'English'.." (I Drink Therefore I Am, p30, Roger Scruton)

How things have now changed thanks to an

entrepreneurial spirit, outstanding winemakers, terroir, and a belief and focus on sustainability and quality. English vineyards are making high quality wines from grape varietals such as Bacchus, Scheurebe, Regent, Rondo that are well suited to the terroir of our green and pleasant land. Then there are the brave few making a success of growing Chardonnay, Pinot Noir and Pinot Meunière, a combination many of you will recognise as used in the vinification of Champagne. Leading the way is Nyetimber, an estate situated on the chalky South Downs of Sussex, whose sparkling wines have been scooping up international wine awards for over a decade now, such as its 2003 vintage winning the sparkling wine category in a 2010 competition in Italy ahead of many well known champagnes. Then in 2018 English winemakers celebrated a spectacular showing at the International Wine Challenge awards dinner, as Nyetimber's Cherie Spriggs and Camel Valley's Bob Lindo won major awards. These are the "Oscars" of the wine world and the top award went to Ms Spriggs, the head winemaker at Nyetimber, who was crowned Sparkling Winemaker of the Year. **She is both the first woman and the first winemaker outside of Champagne to win the award!** Then there is Chapel Down and Winbirri Estates with the latter winning the 2017 Decanter World Wines awards Platinum Medal for its Bacchus 2015 vintage. This was the first English Vineyard to win the international still white wine category. More will come as these stellar examples of English wine inspire many others across the country, including these two examples not far from our own home.

Think Local, Drink Local

1. Poulton Hill

A couple of years ago one of our combined "travels and wine tasting" took us less than 7 miles from our Cotswolds home, and for the first few miles we speculated that this was an April Fool joke and that we'd lost track of time again in our old age! The visit was prompted by a BT/Openreach telephone engineer who, fixing our internal phone wiring, had glimpsed our wine collection, and told us of a vineyard only a couple of villages away. Our doubts increased as we turned left at Poulton village onto the Down Ampney road, and 10 minutes later had reached Down Ampney with no sign of anything to do with wines or vines. We HAD seen a "bloody big house" on our right behind some rather large gates, but nothing to say there was a vineyard there in disguise or in hiding.

Now, let me stop there, because this is not meant to be a negative description of the quite fantastic Poulton Hill Estate, a relatively new vineyard in the Cotswolds just south of Cirencester. A new entrance was about to be opened with a sign to the vineyard and what I had seen at the gates was the entrance to the owners house and guest accommodation. Driving up to the large gates they opened electronically, and after 100 metres or so we turned into the vineyard and Cellar Door tasting room.

Here we were welcomed by Tileri the Managing Director and Natalie the Assistant Manager who enthusiastically described the history, current operation and future of the vineyard, and then the detail of the grape varieties and wines produced. Our blog followers know that we have visited vineyards all over the world, some very large and some very small, but this was the most welcoming and enthusiastic we have received, especially since their wine tours and wine tastings were normally only by appointment at that time.

Their main grapes grown are classically those best suited to our "English terroir", and include Seyval Blanc, Bacchus, Phoenix, Rondo and Pinot Noir. Not a Pinot Grigio or Shiraz in sight, but Phoenix was a new grape to me and I subsequently found it to be a cross species between Bacchus and Villard Blanc, but enough technical stuff and on to the tasting.

Natalie now lined up five wines for me to taste, a still Rose, a Bacchus, a Phoenix, a Rondo, and an English Sparkling Rose. By the way, isn't it time England had its OWN word or brand for "sparkling" that matches Champagne, Prosecco, Cava, or Cremant de ....?

As usual I won't get into detailed tasting notes here (the wine tasting notes on the Poulton Hill Estate website are very good) but each wine was typically fresh and classically English. I would recommend ANY of them, but I found the Bacchus and Rondo to be outstanding and certainly as good as recent wines I had tasted at other English vineyards. However I bought one of each for our family team to taste at our leisure before we planned our return for a "proper purchase expedition".

2. Bothy Vineyard

Bothy is another vineyard local to us, only 23 miles away from our home and over the border from Gloucestershire into Oxfordshire. I've already referred to it in the Wines With Art chapter regarding their Sculpture in the Vineyard Exhibitions, it's one of our English vineyard favourites with a lot of connected history, and here's a sample:

Oxford is the county town of Oxfordshire and famous worldwide for its prestigious university, the oldest in the English-speaking world. In his poem 'Thyrsis' the Victorian poet Matthew Arnold called Oxford 'the city of dreaming spires' after the stunning architecture of these university buildings. Arnold wrote this poem to commemorate the life of his late friend, Arthur Hugh Clough whose most famous work was **The Bothie of Tober-na-Vuolich.**

I hope you're following this and starting to connect Oxford, with Dreaming Spires, Matthew Arnold, Arthur Hugh Clough, The Bothie ....?? Not yet? Then here's a bit more ....

Two rivers run through Oxford, the Cherwell and the Thames (Isis), and it is from this riverside situation that

Oxford got its name in Saxon times, 'Oxenaforda' or 'Ford of the Oxen'. In the 10th century Oxford became an important frontier town between the kingdoms of Mercia and Wessex and was also strategically important to the Normans who in 1071 built a castle there, first in timber then later in the 11th century, in stone. Oxford Castle played an important part in The Anarchy in 1142 when Matilda was imprisoned there, and later, like many other castles, was mostly destroyed during the English Civil War. What has all this got to do with winemaking you must be asking! Here we go then ....

Bothy Vineyard is the oldest vineyard (40+ years) in Oxfordshire and is situated in the parish of Frilford which has two significant archaeological sites: a Roman villa and a cemetery on Frilford Heath that appears to include both Roman and Saxon burials. So, we have an old vineyard in a very old parish of Oxfordshire, England, owned and run by Dr Richard Liwicki, who also works at Oxford University, and his wife Sian. Anyway, enough tenuous and tortuous history connections then, let's get on with the wine!

The grapes grown here are Ortega, Bacchus, Findling, Perle of Alzey, Alba Longa, Huxelrebe (the whites), and Rondo, Regent, Dornfelder (the reds). Their wines are mostly blends of these grapes, although The Doctor's Bacchus is clearly a single varietal wine as is another named wine, Renaissance, which is made from Ortega. Their blended wines are Oxford Dry (Huxelrebe, Findling, Perle) and Oxford Pink (Rondo, Regent, Dornfelder). In addition they have the stunning sparkler, Halcyon Days, which is a pink fizz made from "lots of grapes blended together" Sian has told us.

What really stands out about this vineyard however is its sustainable environment-conscious approach. Richard and Sian are both scientists and unsurprisingly run their vineyard in a very scientific manner, but with a major focus on sustainability. Even within the short amount of time we have spent with Sian it is very obvious how important it is for them that their winemaking integrates totally with the land and the environment overall. In their own words:

"Our philosophy at Bothy Vineyard is to produce the highest quality wines from grapes cultivated in as environmentally friendly a way as possible. We continue an ancient tradition of wine making in the Vale of the White Horse, Oxfordshire. The local micro-climate, warm sandy soils, long ripening season and mature vines produce wines of consistent depth and quality which have won many awards."

We are mightily impressed with Bothy Vineyard, their whole approach resonates with us and as a couple of scientists ourselves we can see how Richard and Sian are making good use of their specific knowledge and education as scientists. Their wines are high quality, and ...... exceptional value which is very difficult with English wines produced in low volume at high cost: Our favourites here are Halcyon Days and Oxford Dry, high quality and high value.

3. Is English sparkling "Bubbling" enough?

English Sparkling Wine is really bubbling at the moment in a marketing sense, brilliant wines being produced in Sussex, Kent, Hampshire, Gloucestershire and more. Nyetimber, Chapel Down, Three Choirs, Poulton Hill to name only a few. But I have a problem .... "English Sparkling Wine", too many words! Think Champagne or Cremant, or Prosecco, or Cava, for France, Italy and Spain. Browse the shelves of any supermarket wine section and Champagne, or Prosecco, or Cava hit you right between the eyes! There ain't no French Sparkling Wine or Italian Sparkling Wine labels cowering in a line, they are absolutely SHOUTING "buy me now" at us in big bold letters. Meanwhile, little old English Sparkling Wine from Sussex is on a bottom shelf somewhere or in a Rest of Europe section.

I believe this is a big issue but nobody seems to be raising it, although the association of English Wine Producers have taken a small step and "protected" the status of English and Welsh wines with PDO and PGI status:

"Protected geographical status has just been introduced for English and Welsh wines. Look for UK still and sparkling wines that are labelled with "Protected Designation of Origin" or "Protected Geographic Indication" – they will have passed certain taste and analytical parameters under wine schemes sponsored by the UKVA, The producers must also prove the geographical origins of the grapes – PDO wines comply with more stringent rules on the origin of their grapes than PGI wines."

Also Andrew Jefford has written about this with his article "Brexit and GIs: Ignore protected names at your peril" and is absolutely correct in focusing on the central issue of "truth telling". If I buy a bottle of Chablis I need to be 100% certain that it's made from Chardonnay and is from Chablis itself. But it's also about branding and marketing, Champagne and Prosecco are basically getting a free ride on our supermarket shelves, we surely need a brand name, a collective name for our English Sparkling Wine!

One suggestion comes from the Poulton Hill Estate in Gloucestershire with the Latin word BULARI meaning ..... bubbles!

"Poulton Hill Estate has trademark registered 'Bulari' (a variation of the Latin for bubbles) as a generic term to describe English sparkling wine. English sparkling wine producers have been searching for a catchy name to signify prestige and reflect ever-increasing quality for years now. The use of the Latin term Bulari reflects the fact that vines for wine-making were first introduced to Britain by the Romans."

So imagine Nyetimber, Chapeldown, Poulton Hill with a protected status of their Bulari, with our wine industry getting behind such a protected brand, even if they don't like that particular suggestion. Time to really fly the flag!

Chapter 21
From Wine Bluff to Wine Buff

Looking back a couple of years, 2018 had been a heck of a year in my personal wine calendar! First, I made it to membership of the Wine Century Club having tasted wines from 100+ different grapes. Then I converted our travel blog into one focusing exclusively on wine …. tasting, travels, philosophy. Third, I began my Wines 101 Bucket List and travelled to Chablis and then Alsace seeking out two particularly difficult to source Grand Cru Wines. And now ………. I get selected as a judge in a Wine Awards event!

"The People's Choice Wine Awards is a wine challenge for supermarkets, importers, producers and retailers. The ethos behind the PCWA is simple – giving the consumer the opportunity to vote for the wines they love means that they are at the heart of the process, rather than being disengaged from it. The terminology and categories have been made easy to understand and meaningful to the average wine drinker. This helps them make better buying decisions and helps retailers understand what their customer wants. The judges are a mixture of professional wine tasters, industry professionals and experienced amateurs"

"Food and wine pairing is bullshit!"

So, I applied to be a judge and bingo, I was selected for the PCWA challenge to be held in Manchester, UK, on October 1st 2018, and as you have read above we were to judge supermarket wines in categories, unusual categories, such as matching wines with barbecued food, spicy food, or for a "girls night out"! Crazy, but interesting!

Wine tasting is as "old as the hills" but still often leads to disagreement between professionals at awards competitions, and confusion amongst novices who either don't understand the tasting notes of the professionals or have completely different experiences. The major issue is being able to discern and discriminate between wines you taste. For example as you experience a variety of wines you will build up your own mental library and be able to discern the difference between a Shiraz, a Cabernet Sauvignon and a Merlot, or between a Sauvignon Blanc, a Chardonnay and a Pinot Grigio. Then as experiences grow you will be able to discriminate between good and less good wines of the same grape, or Pinot Noir wines from Burgundy, New Zealand and California. There is nothing magical about being able to do this, just having lots of different experiences, following our step by step process, and keeping a record. What could be better than an evening with a few friends and 3 different wines but similar in some specific way. Here's a few examples to try:

1. A Sancerre, plus a Sauvignon Blanc from New Zealand and one from USA
2. A red Burgundy, plus a Pinot Noir from New Zealand and one from USA
3. A Chablis plus an unoaked Chardonnay from

Australia, one from New Zealand AND one from
Chile

In this way you could learn how to discern and discriminate between wines of THE SAME grape but different countries, regions, winemakers or vintages/years.

Another issue is one in which we are recommended certain wines to match specific foods which can often lead to great disappointment. Interestingly there is a "famous" Master of Wine, Tim Hanni, who says "Food and Wine Pairing is Bullshit"! No, I didn't make that up and I am not misquoting him because you can read his words in an online article at The Drinks Business Website here (https://www.thedrinksbusiness.com/2019/02/tim-hanni-mw-food-and-wine-pairing-is-bullsht/) The article was written on 19th February 2019 by Lucy Shaw as a follow up to Tim's talk at the 2019 Sauvignon Blanc Celebration in Marlborough in which he had said "A perfect wine pairing doesn't exist. We're doing a lot of damage the way we're matching wine and categorising it. We need to start a campaign to stop wine and food pairing as we've created a lot of bullshit around the idea. We need to get over the notion that food and wine grew up together. Food and wine matching is pseudo science full of metaphors and misunderstandings,"

Now, in his book _Why You Like The Wines You Like_, Tim clarifies and expands on his rather explosive Marlborough talk by describing how we are ALL different in our sensory perceptions of wine, PLUS, how the simple addition of salt or acid in the form of lemon or lime juice to a food can completely alter whether we enjoy a particular wine with a particular food. I have tried this with friends at home, for example adding either condiment to prawns, charcuterie, smoked salmon as they tried a variety of red and white wines before and after the addition. It makes for a very interesting experience, I recommend it as well as buying the book which I just cannot do ample justice to here.

So, back to being a wine judge at the PCWA event in Manchester having read Tim Hanni's book a month earlier and wondering how much it would influence my judgement, in addition to having the personal belief that the best wine to match any food has to be AT LEAST a wine that you enjoy WITHOUT food! I entered the PCWA tasting room with a mix of excitement, curiosity and trepidation.

How did it go?
Many of you reading this will not know of our blog, *Buddha Walks Into A Wine Bar* in which occasionally I write a post describing an incident, a visit, some philosophy, as if in conversation with Buddha. There is no disrespect intended in this, Champa and I are both Buddhists and often discuss and deal with our problems

beginning with "what would Sid say if he were here"? We call him by his birth name, Siddhartha, and so here is a description of my thoughts on the wine judge experience as if in conversation, S is Siddhartha and B is myself.

Sitting in my own "wine room" at home a week later I started to reflect on the hectic couple of days travelling to and from Manchester as a wine judge for the People's Choice Wine Awards, when who should appear but Buddha himself.

B: "Good grief Sid, you shouldn't just appear like that, it's a bit more dramatic than walking into our usual wine bar!"
S: "Sorry Dr B, I thought it was an opportune moment as you seemed deep in thought about your recent wine judging experience" said the Enlightened One.
B: "That's OK Sid, but I'm sure you have a purpose in the visit, as usual?"
S: "Yes, I do …. I'm wondering about how you balanced your mindful/existentialism principles with having to judge something for "others" related to matching a specific food that you weren't sampling at the same time …. if you know what I mean?"
B: "Yes Sid, I know exactly what you mean, and it wasn't easy, especially as in one category we were given about 15 heavy red wines to taste and match/judge for pairing with barbecued food, at a rate of roughly one every 3mins"

S: "What! Only 3mins to savour, experience, be mindful of …. a single wine before deciding the extent to which it paired with the classic burgers, sausages, steaks as opposed to the lightly grilled shrimp or seared tuna or maybe a chicken goujon in a few herbs?"

B: "That's it Sid, you got it in one"

S: "You know Dr B, I once kept a single grape in my mouth for 8 hours without chewing or swallowing it"

B "I read about that Sid, how on earth did you manage it?"

S "I wish you hadn't asked, I fell asleep but nobody ever writes that bit"

"  "

B "Well that's enlightened me on something I didn't know about 5mins ago, but I must admit I did find the leap from describing a wine to passing judgement on it somewhat hard. As you know I have quite a wide experience of tasting many different varieties of wines around the world, often in situ, but I never actually buy a wine because I think it will match a specific food. I certainly consider acidity, minerality, balance, quality and value for money before I buy more of a wine, but only after having concentrated really hard on describing the wine itself and then, and only then, considering whether I like it or not."

S "I think that's very wise and existentialist of you Dr B, Mr Sartre would be proud of you, as am I. Mindfulness should be a skill developed for wine and food tasting, especially given the scale of marketing and selling of wines in supermarkets etc across the world, the sellers have a huge responsibility to use good quality and informative notes from professional wine critics and writers"

B "Yes Sid, but also I strongly believe that the critics and writers have a duty to focus on the end consumer too, not only to taste and report on the wines that score 95/100 and cost a fortune, but to seek out the low cost high value wines ….. and also to avoid the Fruit Salad Bingo descriptions because not everyone can detect 1ppm of a specific ester that reminds them of strawberries or of phenylacetaldehyde that reminds them of ginger."

S "OK, OK, I know you have a PhD in chemistry, how did you ENJOY the experience?"

B "Oh I'm very positive about it. The event was very well organised, the organisers themselves were charming people, and my table group were extremely friendly and all with a passionate love of wine. Everyone worked very hard to be objective, to follow the process and keep to schedule. I've made some extra friends on the social networks too, a couple are regularly in touch. A pity that the winning wines in each category won't be known for a few months yet, that's all."

S "Have patience Grasshopper, there is still much to reflect on and discuss …….."

And now two years later I still see the experience as extremely positive. It was a small window into the world of professional wine tasters who sometimes taste and judge hundreds of wines at a time. How on earth do they do it without getting a "pickled tongue" either after a couple of hours or worse still, permanently? Certainly as I walked back to my hotel in Manchester that evening I didn't want to look at another glass of wine for a while, never mind taste one!

For the PCWA producers, suppliers, retailers and agents are invited to submit their wines and provide details including price, vintage and retail availability. Three bottles of each wine are required and must be sent to the delivery address on the submission form. Round 1 is judged by hand-picked, wine knowledgeable consumers in Manchester. Each table is headed up by two wine-qualified professionals who give basic guidance and explain the judging process. All wines are tasted blind and are judged on a points-based scoring system, rated with the description of the category in mind. This panel produces the shortlist of wines that are then judged in Round 2 at a later date by professional wine judges plus a few selected amateurs from Round 1. Not sure how they selected the amateurs to return and I wasn't one of them, but I didn't mind that at all, nothing can detract from my enjoyment of the evening and the satisfaction I feel to this day. The increase in self esteem having become a "wine buff" will be with me for ever.

Chapter 22
What Was All That About?

What is it that drives someone to write a book, especially a book which exposes some innermost thoughts and experiences in a personal memoir? "Why am I writing this" has been a constant voice in my head as I scribbled, typed, proofread, chose images and ploughed through the technical details of self publishing on Amazon. It certainly wasn't a financial issue driven by a personal need for money. Nor has it been a psychological issue driven by a need for achievement or recognition. But having reached the final chapter I can now recognise that it has been an emotional or affective issue, maybe better expressed as a labour of love to recollect, collate and then share with fellow winos a torrent of experiences in this book. What could be better than reflecting positively on the 50 years of wine related experiences that were all shared with one's wife and children, and now sharing them with fellow winos, new and old? The ancient Greeks got it right with their Symposium in which they met over dinner, with wine of course, and engaged in conversation, poetry, music, and philosophical discussion as a tribute to Dionysus, continued by the Romans in honour of the same god they named Bacchus. Wine can be a catalyst for a civilised engagement with our fellow man rather than a route to intoxication over a noisy argumentative dinner table, or worse still drunken behaviour in the streets after the bars have closed! Equally there is a vast new world of wine to discover out there by venturing beyond the impersonal nature of the supermarket shelves, instead stepping into the specialist wine merchant, the vineyard, the wine cooperative, or the wine club. And as you meet new people and make new friends you will find new interests that enhance your understanding and appreciation of wine, just as we did, including art, history, philosophy. It all depends where the wine takes you.

So I want to end this book by sharing with you a few of the major areas of knowledge and learning that have been gained across these 50 years. All of them we now "carry around" with us as we travel to Burgundy, walk into a local English vineyard, enter a nearby wine bar, or scan the shelves of our village wine merchant.

1. My Priests of Bacchus

Modern definitions of the adjective "Bacchanalian" allude to "drunken revelry", drinking lots of alcohol and uncontrolled behaviour. But none of these definitions mean anything to me. Bacchus is the Roman version of the Ancient Greek god of wine, Dionysus, and is also a grape, a named wine of England especially notable from the award winning Winbirri vineyard in Norfolk, a vine growing in my garden, and the subject of a painting by Caravaggio. The Ancient Greeks at the time of Plato honoured Dionysus through their Symposium, a gathering of men who after dinner would continue with wine as they discussed politics, read poetry, played and listened to music, all in appreciation of their god.

As outlined above the notion of the Greek Symposium has also been part of my own engagement with wine. During the past 50 years I consider myself fortunate to have had three "priests of Bacchus", two of whom I have never met, but each has influenced how I buy, drink, appreciate and think about wine.

The first priest was the late Professor John Ottaway of the University of Strathclyde, possibly the greatest analytical chemist of his era. John was my PhD supervisor in the 60s, a good friend with an interest in wine, mountains, bird watching, classical music and fine dining. I had my first EVER bottle of wine with him, it was a Portuguese Vinho Verde, a young "green" wine made from local grapes and slightly petillant in nature. There would be many more over the next few years, we even made wine together, and our personal conversations were typically philosophical and cultural rather than the academic chemistry conversations in which we challenged each other beyond belief. The wine healed all wounds, he died young and I miss him greatly.

The second priest I never met, the late great English philosopher Sir Roger Scruton. His book *I Drink Therefore I Am* has been a revelation and a constant companion on our travels as well as on long walks in the Cotswolds countryside. I have all three formats, Kindle, Hardback and Audible which seems crazy but it lets me dip into it in different environments. The book has a mixture of wine history, wine politics, wine tasting and philosophical questions about the subjectivity of the aroma and taste of wine. We seem to have shared, quite separately of course, an identical chapter of time in which we drank many of the same wines, visited similar places, appreciate the value of terroir, admire the same vignerons, and believe in the local over the global not only in wine but in many other issues. Sir Roger died in December 2019 and the world is a poorer place without this patriotic great modern philosopher.

My third priest is really a priestess and, thankfully, still alive! Danell Nelson is a young American woman, a qualified sommelier living near Naples in Italy. We "met" through our respective blogs with hers focusing more on the aesthetic nature of wine often using art as the medium, compared to mine which is often sceptical, irreverent and highly critical of wine professionals. We have disagreed on many things wine related, especially the subjective vs objective issue of wine tasting, and the ability or lack of it to taste or smell that "fruit salad bingo" of descriptions used by many wine professionals. And yet here we are two years later with Danell designing the cover of this book and collaborating with me in writing the chapter Wine with Art. We communicate through emails and FaceTime video calls .... It REALLY isn't about the wine, but about the same appreciation of Dionysus/Bacchus as held by those in the Greek Symposium.

2. I'm a Terroiriste!

For many years now it has been unfashionable to buy, drink, think about or consider wine as anything other than an alcoholic drink made from whatever the varietal name on the label. "I'll have a glass of Chardonnay please, how about you, oh I'll have a large Pinot Noir!" said the couple in a fashionable London wine bar. Meanwhile, at the next table, having called the waiter over, one person asks for a Chablis Premier Cru Fourchaume, the other asks for a Pommard Premier Cru Les Rugiens. The second couple care about where their wine comes from and what it tastes like, one is a chardonnay the other is a pinot noir, they are terroiristes. The first couple are garagistes, they neither know nor care about where the wine comes from or about the skill that has gone into making it. The first pair are globalists and support and pay for the large corporations who blend and control production of wine like it's a can of baked beans. Every can must taste the same. The second pair are localists. They respect the traditional winemaker who nurtures his vines and produces a wine that is not only distinct compared to another region, but distinct from a neighbours wine produced from the opposite side of the hill! Think local, drink local and have infinite choice and an infinite variety of styles even for a single grape. I am a rampant terroiriste and would never consider buying or drinking a wine that had been blended and "twisted" to suit a global market. And slowly but surely all over the world terroir is being championed in Argentina, Oregon, New Zealand, Australia and ..... England. Time to join us and seek out wines that are terroir driven.

3. I'm a Sensitive Vinotype!

Can you tell much about a person based on the wine they drink? If personality can be inferred from our behaviour, and wine choice is part of our behaviour then there should be some connection. Don't just take my word for it, this is one of the important concepts in Tim Hanni's book *Why You Like The Wines You Like* in which he describes four "vinotypes" who each respond to wine in different ways. Tim and his colleagues explored the psychological and physiological factors that contribute to our personal preferences, particularly the physiological factors of our sensitivity to different tastes and flavours. They developed a questionnaire which *"consists of various questions that help us determine your physiological boundaries – your sensory sensitivities and tolerances. Next comes your genre, which is an expression of the elements you value about wine. The final step is to simply declare the kind of wines you favor – be it sweet and pink or intense and red, or anywhere in between."* The result of the assessment is your Vinotype, placing you as one of Sweet, Hypersensitive, Sensitive, or Tolerant.

Taking the full questionnaire I was assessed as a **Sensitive** with wine preference characteristics including the following:

- Most satisfied with more delicate wines (Yes, Pinot Noir rather than Cabernet Sauvignon for example, light Chablis rather than big Aussie chardonnays)
- Tends to seek wines with balance (Yes, I am constantly sensing whether there is balance across fruit, tannin and acidity in a wine which I almost always write into my tasting notes)
- Adventurous and open to trying different wine styles but NOT heavily oaked (Yes, constantly seeking terroir driven differences in Pinot Noir and Chardonnay but can't stand oaked wines)
- Places high importance in wine complexity (Yes, always a feature of my tasting notes)

There isn't space here to describe the Vinotype concept in more detail, but I include this brief description here because it contributes to how I have evolved as a wine lover, why I like certain wines, why terroir driven wines are the ones I seek out and why wine adventure and curiosity has grown as I have aged. In essence it helped me to understand my preferences and stop mentally beating myself up because I was constantly seeking the holy grail of a better Pinot Noir than the one I had just drunk.

Taste isn't everything!
A couple of years ago I bought a book called

Neuroenology; How the Brain Creates the Taste of Wine by Gordon M Shepherd, the professor of neuroscience at Yale School of Medicine. It is the first book on wine tasting written by a neuroscientist and, having degrees in chemistry and psychology and a hobby of wine collecting, it was an absolute no-brainer to buy it. I'm glad I did, because it revealed to me something that has explained so much about my lack of ability to "taste" many of the flavours in wine and also completely changed HOW I go about tasting a wine in the first place.

Shortly after the book had been published it seemed to me that the professional wine fraternity completely glossed over some key findings. In fact they had been almost frivolous in their reporting with "headlines" about "how wine tasting isn't all in your head" or "how tasting wine stimulates brain-maths" or "how wine tasting stimulates your brain more than any other behaviour such as listening to music". They missed a great opportunity to help all of us wine lovers to not only enjoy wines more, but to understand how we can better choose wines to drink, how we can "find the right language" to describe a wine or even to relate better to wine waiters or sommeliers. Wouldn't you like to know some of these things? Shouldn't the wine profession have acted more openly and responsibly? Well, maybe I'm being a little harsh, but I suspect that most of them hadn't even read Shepherd's book in any depth. The core of the book is complex, naturally, but I bought it as not only a wine lover but also as a scientist and a psychologist. But don't worry, I'm not going to review here the neural pathways and brain centres involved! It's all about the wine.

- The book begins with sections on "The Fluid

Dynamics of Wine Tasting". If you thought that just getting a mouthful of wine, swirling it around a bit then swallowing is the be-all-and-end-all of wine tasting …. think again! Between lips and gut there is a flow of liquid and aromas involving 7 steps and multiple muscles, cavities and organs such as tongue, soft palate, vallecula, epiglottis, esophagus , and numerous receptor cells. …… that's all you need to remember!

- **The most significant element of the Fluid Dynamics section is that there are TWO types of "smell" the Orthonasal (breathing in through the nose) and the Retronasal (breathing out through the nose).** In a simplified way, orthonasal occurs just before we take a sip of wine and retronasal occurs just after swallow. The latter is hardly noticeable, almost an unconscious action. Try it, sip some wine and see if you can sense each happening? They each play a part of differing significance in our tasting experience.

- Did you sense a retronasal breath after swallowing? Did you experience any aromas? Were those aromas different in any way from the orthonasal inward sniff? The aromas involved from the retronasal breath are quite different from the orthonasal for several different reasons including how the wine has now been agitated around the mouth, how it has been mixed with saliva, and that new volatiles have been created. Professor Shepherd highlights this as MOST significant!

- **Wine taste is not actually taste, it is retronasal smell that we mostly experience and identify as**

taste! I'll say that again but quoting Shepherd's own words: "{once the wine is swallowed} retronasal smell dominates ….. the aroma burst and the finish", and "there is a clear implication that retronasal smell is the prime driver …… in the after-taste period". Staggering isn't it, most of our sensory experience of a wine comes from nasal receptors after swallowing and NOT from the tongue or palate or throat!

- Is this why the "experts" taste a myriad of things that a humble amateur like myself never gets? Cherry, tobacco, mushroom, citrus, gooseberry, even leather and sweaty saddle! It has been quite frustrating at times to attend wine tastings and to say "it tastes of Chardonnay" and then to be asked "but what do you taste, do you get butteriness or honey ….?" Utterly infuriating.

- Professor Shepherd does explain this too saying **"it's our brain that creates the "taste" " and that each person is different in terms of things like amount of saliva produced as well as previous stored memories of tastes etc.** But the difficulty we have is moving from perception to language, the words to describe that taste. Description is different from evaluation or judgement, so saying "honey and oak" is different descriptively from saying "acidic I don't like it". I saw this on a wine tv show recently where a UK wine expert was trying to guide a group of Chinese people through tasting some Burgundy Pinot Noir wines. They couldn't identify with cherry, raspberry, earthy etc. But everything changed when the discussion switched to perceiving the wine taste as types of Chinese tea flavours such as puerh, oolong, keemun, etc. These were now Chinese memories, NOT UK wine expert memories using so many brain centres each with their own function.

So what does all of this mean and how does it add to our enjoyment of wine and wine tasting? Personally I now focus a lot more on a slight retronasal "out breath" after the first sip, taking my time to understand, describe and evaluate my perception. By doing this I sense far more aromas and flavours and for a longer period than ever before.I focus my sense of smell on only three things..Fruitiness, Floweriness, Earthiness. I focus my sense of taste on Fruit, Acidity, Tannin. And finally I evaluate the wine in terms of Finish (short, medium, long) before giving it a score based on 1-5 stars related to how much I liked it.

Not everyone has this "Jedi-like" mind or perceives a myriad of aromas on first sniffing or tasting a wine and are constantly baffled at the cherries, lemon, cigar box, chocolate, leather, kiwi fruit, list of descriptions of particular sensations. It's a personal thing, like the Chinese subjects in the wine tasting session who were also utterly baffled at the western tutor's use of fruits, flowers etc in describing a wine. But when the Chinese assistant started to add in some descriptions related to different teas and their tannins, all of the mental light bulbs came on! Professor Shepherd's book helps us to understand the whole wine tasting process better and can add a great deal to all wine lovers and their wine travels! It added to mine and I hope it will add to yours.

But remember ....

"At the end of the day, what matters is never the wine, it's always the moment; it's always the people."
(Olivier Magny, Into Wine: An Invitation to Pleasure)

References & Links

Chapter 1
It's Not About The Wine

1. Kent Bach, "What good is knowledge in enjoying the experience of wine"
(http://www.wineanorak.com/philosophy_of_wine2.htm)

2. Domaine du Closel, Savennieres, Loire, France
(http://www.savennieres-closel.com/?lang=en)

3. Pierre & Bertrand Couly, Chinon, Loire, France
(https://pb-couly.com)

Chapter 2
Early Learning

1. Chateauneuf du Pape, Fete de la Veraison, Rhone, France
(https://www.chateauneuf-du-pape-tourisme.fr/fr/liste/fête-de-la-véraison)

2. Gratien & Meyer, Saumur, Loire, France
(https://www.gratienmeyer.com/en/)

Chapter 3
Wine & Travel Connections

1. Miramar Restaurant, Bedar, Murcia, Spain

(https://www.tripadvisor.co.uk/Restaurant_Review-g580275-d788496-Reviews-Miramar-Bedar_Province_of_Almeria_Andalucia.html)

2. The Five EssentialCharacteristics of a Wine Lover, Alder Yarrow, Vinography,
(https://www.vinography.com/2020/04/the_five_virtues_of_a_wine_lov)

Chapter 4
Fruit Salad Bingo

1. "Some nifty science to help you understand wine aromas", Andrea Buffer
(https://winefolly.com/deep-dive/some-science-to-wine-aromas/)

2. Avery Gilbert, "What the Nose Knows: The Science of Scent in Everyday Life" (Crown, New York; 2008), pp.233–34.)

3. Leigh Francis et al., "Pepper and Spice in Shiraz"
(https://www.awri.com.au/wp-content/uploads/2013/08/francis-W07pepper-AWITC15.pdf)

4. Why You Like The Wines You Like, Tim Hanni, ISBN-13 : 978-0615750880

Chapter 6
2015 Loire-Chinon

1. Hotel Le Plantagenet, 12 Place Jeanne d'Arc, 37500 Chinon, France

2. Kermit Lynch Wines (https://www.kermitlynch.com/our-wines/charles-joguet/)

3. Cave des Silenes, 43 Avenue François Mitterrand, 37500 Chinon, France (http://www.cavedessilenes.com/en/)

4. A la Pause Rabelaisienne, 28 Place du General de Gaulle, 375000, Chinon, France

5. La Cave Voltaire, 13 Rue Voltaire, 37500 Chinon, France

6. Cafe De La Paix, 6-2 Ile de Tours, 37500 Chinon, France

7. Hotel La Croix Blanche, 7 Place des Plantagenets, 49590

Fontevraud-l'Abbaye, France

Chapter 7
2016 Alsace-Turckheim

1. L'Auberge du Brand, 8 Grand'rue, 68230 Turckheim, France

2. Cave de Turckheim, 16 Rue des Tuileries, 68230 Turckheim, France
https://www.cave-turckheim.com/gb/

3. Francois Baur, 3 Grand'rue, 68230 Turckheim, France
https://www.vinsbaur.com/en/

4. Brasserie de la Poste, 1 Place de la 1E Armée, 68150 Ribeauvillé, France

Chapter 8
2016 Burgundy-Pommard

1. Holiday Lettings Pommard les Charmots apartment (https://www.holidaylettings.co.uk/rentals/pommard/6895781?rSid=sp8)

2. Cellier Volnaysien, Volnay
(https://www.restaurant-lecelliervolnaysien.com/en/)

3. Domaine Francois Gaunoux, Meursault
(https://www.gaunoux.com/en/)

4. Cave des Vignerons de Buxy, Buxy
(http://www.vigneronsdebuxy.fr/index.php?
page=actu&lang=fr&actu=85)

5. The Wine Society review of the Vignerons de Buxy
(https://www.thewinesociety.com/grower-profile-caves-
de-vignerons-de-buxy)

6. The World Atlas of Wine, (Mitchell Beazley) Hugh
Johnson & Jancis Robinson

7. Auberge des Vignes, Volnay
http://www.aubergedesvignes.fr

8. Le Grand Cafe de Lyon, Beaune
36 Place Carnot, 21200 Beaune, France

9. Bar 66, Beaune
30 Place Carnot, 21200 Beaune, France

10. Athenaeum, Beaune

5 Rue de l'Hôtel Dieu, 21200 Beaune, France

https://www.athenaeum.com

11. Hotel-Dieu, The Hospices de Beaune, Beaune

https://www.beaune-tourism.com/discover/the-hospices-de-beaune

12. Alain Hess, 7 Place Carnot, 21200, Beaune

https://fromageriealainhess.com/fr/

Chapter 9
2017 Burgundy-Meursault

1. Chez Hall - La Grande Maison,

https://www.holidaylettings.co.uk/rentals/meursault/6889737

2. Patriarche Pere & Fils, 5-7 Rue du Collège/r Paul Chanson, 21200 Beaune, France

https://www.patriarche.com

3. Domaine Francois Gaunoux, Meursault

(https://www.gaunoux.com/en/)

4. Caveau de Puligny-Montrachet, 1 Rue de Poiseul, 21190 Puligny-Montrachet, France

http://www.caveau-puligny.com

5. L'Estaminet des Meix, Place du pasquier De la fontaine, 21190 Puligny-Montrachet, France

6. Puligny-Montrachet: Journal of a Village in Burgundy, Simon Loftus.

https://www.amazon.co.uk/Puligny-Montrachet-Journal-Burgundy-Simon-Loftus/dp/1911547488/ref=mp_s_a_1_2?
dchild=1&keywords=puligny+montrachet&qid=159876574
9&s=digital-text&sr=1-2

7. Château de la Rochepot, 21340 La Rochepot, France

www.chateau-de-la-rochepot.com

Chapter 10
Grapes, Wines & Bottles

1. The Wine Century Club

https://winecentury.com

2. 101 Wines To Try Before You Die, Margaret Rand,

https://www.amazon.co.uk/101-Wines-try-before-you/
dp/1788400526/ref=tmm_hrd_swatch_0?
_encoding=UTF8&qid=1599130348&sr=1-2

Chapter 11
2018 Burgundy-Chablis

1. The Sommelier's Atlas of Taste, Rajat Parr & Jordan
Mackay,
https://www.amazon.co.uk/dp/B078QRQQ3W/ref=dp-
kindle-redirect?_encoding=UTF8&btkr=1

2. Chablis Bar, 2 rue du Maréchal de Lattre de Tassigny,
89800 Chablis, France

3. Bistro des Grand Crus , 10 Rue Jules Rathier, 89800
Chablis, France

4. Cafe La Chablisienne, 2 Place Charles de Gaulle, 89800
Chablis, France

5. Domaine Des Malandes, 63 Rue Auxerroise, 89800
Chablis, France

6. Domaine Pinson, 5 Quai Voltaire, 89800 Chablis, France

7. La Chablisienne, 8 Boulevard Pasteur, 89800 Chablis, France

Chapter 12
2018 Alsace-Ribeauville

1. Domaine Weinbach, 25 Route du Vin, 68240 Kaysersberg, France

2. Hotel de La Tour, 1 Rue de la Mairie, 68150 Ribeauvillé, France

3. Winstub La Flammerie, 9 Grand'Rue, 68150 Ribeauvillé, France

4. Cave de Ribeauville, 2 Route de Colmar, 68150 Ribeauvillé, France

5. Maison Trimbach, 2 Route de Colmar, 68150 Ribeauvillé, France

Chapter 13
2018 Loire, Fontevraud-l'Abbeye

1. Domaine du Closel, Chateau Des Vaults, 1 Place du Mail,

49170 Savennières, France

2. Hotel La Croix Blanche Fontevraud, 7 Place des Plantagenets, 49590 Fontevraud-l'Abbaye, France

3. Au Clos de l'Echo- Vignobles Couly-Dutheil, Parking du Château, Avenue François Mitterrand, 37500 Chinon, France

4. A la Pause Rabelaisienne, 28 Place du Général de Gaulle, 37500 Chinon, France

5. Chateau de Montreuil-Bellay, Place des Ormeaux, 49260 Montreuil-Bellay, France

6. La Barbacane, 76 Place des Ormeaux, 49260 Montreuil-Bellay, France

7. Chateau de Breze, Bellevigne-les-Chateaux, 20 Rue de l'Amiral Maillé Brézé, 49260 Brézé, France

8. Domaine Henry Pelle, 18220 Morogues, France

9. Domaine Filliatreau, Route de Montsoreau, 49730 Turquant, France

10. Chateau de Saumur, Esplanade Hubert-Landais, 49400 Saumur, France

11. Le Grand Bleu, 6 Rue du Marché, 49400 Saumur, France

Chapter 14
2018 Burgundy, Chablis-Beaune

1. Hostellerie des Clos, 18 Rue Jules Rathier, 89800, Chablis, France

2. Les Trois Bougeons, 10 Rue Auxerrois, 89800 Chablis, France

3. Hotel de La Cloche, 42 Rue du Faubourg Madeleine, 21200 Beaune, France

4. Bar Le Cercle, 39 Rue d'Alsace, 21200 Beaune, France

5. Chateau du Clos de Vougeot, Rue de la Montagne, 21640 Vougeot, France

6. La Grande Cave de Vougeot, 31 Rue du Vieux Château, 21640 Vougeot, France

7. Hotel Vendangerot, Place Sainte-Marie, 71150 Rully, France

Chapter 15
Wine and Celestial Bodies

1. Alder Yarrow, Vinography, https://www.vinography.com

2. World Atlas of Wine, Hugh Johnson & Jancis Robinson, ISBN-13 : 978-1784724030

3. The Oxford Companion to Wine, Jancis Robinson & Julia Harding, ISBN-13 : 978-0198705383

4. Rudolf Steiner, https://www.biodynamics.com/steiner.html

5. An Introduction to Biodynamics, http://www.wineanorak.com/biodynamic1.htm

Chapter 16
Wine with Philosophy

1. At The Existentialist Cafe, Sarah Bakewell, ISBN-13 : 978-0099554882

2. Travels With Epicurus, Daniel Klein, ISBN-13 : 978-0143121930

3. I Drink Therefore I Am: A philosopher's guide to wine, Roger Scruton, ISBN-13 978-1847065087

4. A Short Philosophy of Wine, Neel Burton, https://www.psychologytoday.com/us/blog/hide-and-seek/201805/short-philosophy-wine

Chapter 17
Wine with History

1. L'Imaginarium, Avenue du Jura, 21700 Nuits-Saint-Georges, France

2. The History of Wine in 100 Bottles: From Bacchus to Bordeaux and Beyond, Oz Clarke, ISBN-13 : 978-1909815490

3. Chateau de Clos de Vougeot, Rue de la Montagne, 21640 Vougeot, France

4. Hospice de Beaune, Rue de l'Hotel Dieu, 212000 Beaune, France

5. Blandy's Wine Lodge, Av. Arriaga 28, 9000-064 Funchal, Portugal

Chapter 18
Wine with Art

1. Danell Nelson, www.vinthropology.wordpress.com

2. Bothy Vineyard, Faringdon Rd, Abingdon OX13 6QW, Oxfordshire, England

3. The Wines of Gala, Hans Werner Holzwarth, ISBN-13 : 978-3836567725

4. The Heart of Buddha's Teaching: Transforming suffering into peace, joy and liberation. Thich Nhat Hanh, **ISBN-13 : 978-0712670036**

Chapter 19
2019 Loire, Chinon

1. Citotel Le Plantagenet, 12 Place Jeanne d'Arc, 37500 Chinon, France

2. Travels With Epicurus, Daniel Klein, ISBN-13 :

978-1780744124

3. Gratien & Meyer, Route de Montsoreau, 49400 Saumur, France

4. Brasserie de La Bourse, 1 Place de la Bilange, 49400 Saumur, France

5. Musee Rabelais, 4 Rue de la Devinière, 37500 Seuilly, France

Chapter 20
England!

1. Erode protected names at your peril: Decanter, Andrew Jefford, https://www.decanter.com/magazine/brexit-gi-protected-wine-names-394580/

2. Nyetimber Vineyard, Gay Street, West Chiltington RH20 2HH

3. Winbirri Vineyards, Bramerton rd, Surlingham NR14 7DE

4. Chapel Down Tenterden Vineyard Park, Small Hythe Rd,

Tenterden TN30 7NG

5. Poulton Hill Estate, Poulton, Cirencester GL7 5JA

6. Bothy Vineyard, Faringdon Rd, Abingdon OX13 6QW

Chapter 21
From Wine Bluff to Wine Buff

1. People's Choice Wine Awards, https://peopleschoicedrinksawards.com/pcwa/home/

2. Food And Wine Pairing is Bullshit, https://www.thedrinksbusiness.com/2019/02/tim-hanni-mw-food-and-wine-pairing-is-bullsht/

3. Why You Like The Wines You Like, Tim Hanni, ISBN-13 : 978-0615750880

Chapter 22
What Was That All About

1. Into Wine: An Invitation to Pleasure, Oliver Magny, ISBN-13 : 978-0615658438

2. Neuroenology: How the Brain Creates the Taste of Wine, Gordon M Shepherd, ISBN-13 : 978-0231177009

3. Why You Like The Wines You Like, Tim Hanni, ISBN-13 : 978-0615750880

4. I Drink Therefore I Am: A philosopher's guide to wine, Roger Scruton, ISBN-13 978-1847065087

About the Author

Dr Brian Metters was born in April 1947 in the tiny village of Haverigg, Cumbria, England. Despite leaving school at 16 and working in the local ironworks he studied chemistry at night school before making his way to University of Strathclyde, Glasgow, in 1969. Five years later he had an MSc., and a PhD in analytical chemistry. Brian also met Champa from Kathmandu at Strathclyde and they completed their doctorates together before marrying in 1971.

Brian's early career followed a scientific path for the next 10 years before he decided to "re-educate" as a psychologist and he eventually specialised in Organisation Psychology. After 12 years employed in the financial sector he set up his own consultancy business focused on organisation development work in the banking and insurance industry.

Eventually Brian and Champa retired in 2007 and set up a U.K. charity Nepal Schools Aid initially working with a number of the poorest schools in Kathmandu. In 20012 they created an NGO in Kathmandu, Nepal Education Leadership Foundation with 8 highly trained Nepalese staff. Across the next 5 years they trained 2000 teachers in child centred learning techniques and developed 200 schools in Kathmandu before closing the charity.

Brian's early interests were in mountaineering and ice climbing in the Alps and Himalaya, nowadays his main interest is in wine collecting .... and drinking the stuff, especially Pommard, Volnay, Chablis and Meursault. He is currently "exploring" English vineyards and wines.

Printed in Great Britain
by Amazon

54838474R00183